Hannah M. Reynolds

So Much of the Diary of Lady Willoughby as Relates to her Domestic History

Hannah M. Reynolds

So Much of the Diary of Lady Willoughby as Relates to her Domestic History

ISBN/EAN: 9783337017682

Printed in Europe, USA, Canada, Australia, Japan

Cover: Foto ©ninafisch / pixelio.de

More available books at **www.hansebooks.com**

THE DIARY OF LADY

WILLOUGHBY.

So much of the *DIARY* of
LADY WILLOUGHBY
as relates to her *Domeſtic Hiſtory*, &
to the Eventful Period of the Reign
of Charles the Firſt, the
Protectorate, and the
Reſtoration.

Imprinted for Longmans, Green, Reader,
and Dyer, *Paternoſter Row*, over
againſt *Warwick Lane*, in the
City of London.
1873.

LOAN STACK

To the Reader.

The ſtyle of Printing and general appearance of this Volume have been adopted by the Publiſhers in accordance with the deſign of the Author, who in this Work perſonates a lady of the ſeventeenth Century.

Some Passages from the Diary of Lady

Willoughby.

1635.

1635.

May 12, *Tuesday.*

Rose at my usual houre, six of the clock, for the first time since the Birth of my little *Sonne;* opened the Casement, and look'd forth upon the Park; a herd of Deer pass'd bye, leaving the traces of their Footsteps in the dewy Grasse. The Birds sang, and the Aire was sweet with the scent of the Wood-binde and the fresh Birch Leaves. Took down my *Bible;* found the Mark at the 103d *Psalm;* read the same, and return'd Thanks to *Almighty God* that he had brought me safely through my

1635.

late Peril and Extremity, and in his great Bountie had given me a deare little One. Pray'd him to assist me by his Divine Grace in the right performance of my new and sacred Duties: truly I am a young Mother, and need Help. Sent a Message to my *Lord*, that if it so pleased him, I would take Breakfast with him in the *Blue Parlour*. At Noon walked out on the *South Terrace*; the two Greyhounds came leaping towards me: divers household Affaires in the course of the Day; enough wearied when Night came.

May 19, Tuesday.

Had a disturbed Night, and rose late, not down till after seven: Thoughts wandering at Prayers. The *Chaplain* detained us after Service to know our Pleasure concerning the Christening; my *Lord* doth wish nothing omitted that should seem proper to signify his Respect to that religious Ordinance which admits his *Child* into the outward and visible Church of *Christ*, and give honour to his firste born *Sonne*. During Breakfast we gave the Subject much Consideration. My *Husband* doth not desire him to be named after himself, but rather after his *Father;* his Brother *William* therefore bearing his name will stand Godfather. All being at last brought to a satisfactory conclusion: he went forth with the *Chaplain* and gave his orders according therewith, I doing the same in my smaller capacity: he for whom was all this care lying unconsciously in his Nurse's arms.

Messenger from *Wimbledon*. My deare and honoured *Mother* writes that she doth at present intend setting forth on Monday: gave orders for the *East Chamber* to be prepared. The day being fine walked down to the Dairy; told *Cicely* to make Cheese as often as will suit, the whey being much approved by my *Mother*. The brindled Cow calved yesterday: Calf to be reared, as *Cicely* tells me the mother is the best milker we have. Daisy grows and promises to be a fine Cow: praised *Cicely* for the cleane and orderly state of all under her care; she is a good clever Lasse. As I returned to the house mett my *Lord*, who had come to seeke me; two Strangers with him: thought as he drew near how comely was his countenance: he advanced a pace or two before the others, took my hand, and pressed it to his Lips as he turned and introduced me to Sir *Arthur Hazelrigge* & the Lord *Brooke*: methought the latter very pleasing, of gracefull carriage,

From the Diary of

1635.

and free from any courtly foppery and extravagance in his apparel. They prefently renew'd their converfation refpecting *New England*. Lord *Brooke* and Lord *Say and Sele* have fent over Mr. *George Fenwicke* to purchafe land and commence building: there is talk of Mr. *John Hampden* joining them. Lord *Brooke* difcourfed at length on the admirable qualities and excellent attainements of the late Lord, his coufin, who did come by a cruell death, being murdered by his fervant through a jealoufy he entertained that his paft fervices were neglected. Some Members of my *Lords* Family knew him well, and did fee much of him when Sir *Fulke Greville:* he was greatly efteemed by many, but known chiefly as the Friend and Lover of Sir *Philip Sydney*, whofe early death was mourned by all *England;* and whofe like may not againe be look'd upon. He left directions their friendfhip fhould be recorded on his Tomb, as may be feene in *Warwick Church: Fulke* GREVILLE *Servant to Queen Elizabeth Counfellor to King James and Friend to Sir* PHILIP SYDNEY.

May 25, Monday.

Moft unhappy in mind this day; temper forely tried, and feelings of refentment at what did appeare unkind conduct in another, were too visibly expressed in manner and countenance, though I did refraine from words.

 Slept last night in very Wearinesse of Weeping; and awaken'd this morning with a feeling of Hopelessnesse; and ill at ease myselfe, methought every Thing around seemed melancholy; Truth and Affection doubted, Shortcomings hardly judged of; this is an unlook'd for triall. The Sun shon brightly through the open Window, but it seem'd not to shine for me: I took my *Bible* to read therein my usuall Portion; and kneel'd down to pray, but could only weep: thoughts of my *Mother's* tender love arose, and the Trust on either side that had been unbroken between us. Remembering an outward Composure must be attain'd unto, before I could go down to breakfast, washed my eyes, and let the fresh aire blow upon my face; felt I was a poore dissembler, having had heretofore but little trouble of heart to conceal: mett my *Husband* in the *Corridor* with Lord *Brooke*, and well nigh lost my Selfe-command when he gave a kindly pressure of my Hand as he led me down stairs. This Evening how different does all appear; and though this and some other late Experiences occasion me to perceave that Life is not so calm

1635.

May 26, *Tuesday*.

1635.

a Sea as it once did feeme in my ignorance of humane Nature; flight Breezes may ruffle it, and unfeene Rocks may give a Shock to the little Shipp: haply the Mariner will learn to fteer his courfe, and not feare Shipwreck from every accident.

June 4, Thurfday.

My deare *Mother* arrived at Noon; fhe was fatigued, and retired to her Chamber, firft coming with me to the Nurfery to fee her *Grandfon*; he was awake, and fmiling; fhe took him in her arms and look'd fondly on him. It is a fweet Child, my *Daughter:* may the *Lord* have you both in his fafe Keeping now and evermore. My *Mother's* Bleffing from her own Lips, how precious. She much commends my nurfing him; and would not for my own fake I fhould lofe fo great fatisfaction. I attended her to her Room, where *Mabel* was in waiting: deare kind old *Mabel*, I was well pleafed to fee her, and kiff'd her as I was wont when a Girl; and fo did fpoile a moft refpectfull curtefie to my Ladyfhip. Deare *Mother* look'd round the Room pleafed therewith; and with fuch fmall Comforts as I had been enabled to provide, which fhe hath at home. This Day hath been one of much Happineffe: Returned heart-felt Thanks to

God for his loving Kindneſſe and tender Mercy; read the 23rd *Pſalm*: my Cup doth indeed run over.

    The Houſe full of Company ſince the Chriſtening; and I have felt too weary at night to do more than collect my Thoughts for Devotion. To-day many have left; and my *Huſband* doth purpoſe to begin his Journey to-morrow. My *Mother* with me, he leaveth Home with more eaſe of Mind.

    My deare *Lord* ſet forth at a little paſt ſix, with only one Serving-man, who had a led Horſe and one to carry the baggage. After they had rode ſome way, they ſtopp'd, and my *Lord* diſmounted, and taking a ſhort cut thro' the Park, came up to the Window where I had remain'd to watch his Departure: he bade me call the *Steward*, gave him ſome directions; then telling me to keep up a good heart, took another tender Leave, and followed by *Armſtrong*, returned to the ſpot where were the Horſes; and he mounting the led Horſe, they were ſoon out of ſight. Old *Britton* ſeemed to underſtand he was not to follow his Maſter, and came and reared himſelfe up to the Window, reſting his Fore-paws on the ſtone: I patted his broad Head, and queſtioned not

1635.

June 19, Friday.

1635.

that he felt as I did, that his best Friend was gone: tooke a few turns with him on the *Terrace*; the Mist cleared off the distant Woods and Fields, and I plainly discern'd the Towers of *Framlingham Castle*, and could heare the pleasant sound of the Scythe cutting through the thick Grasse in the fields nearest, and the Cuckoo, as she fled slowly from hedge to hedge.

June 27, Saturday.

Have been greatly fatigued the past Day or two: it is a serious Charge to be left head over so large a Household, but it availeth not to be over carefull. *John Armstrong* knoweth his Lord's Pleasure in most things, and is honest and faithfull: and the *Chaplain* will keep some oversight: and his Counsel in Difficulties, should such arise, may be depended on, though he hath not *John's* Experience in the Family and its Requirements. My Room last night look'd lonely; and *Baby* sleeping somewhat uneasily, I sent for *Nurse*, who stay'd till we were comfortably asleep. I think to have a Truckle bed made up for her; the Room is spacious. Read to-night in *St. John*, chapter 5, and the 93d *Psalm*.

July 5, Sunday.

Feare at times that my Mind is too much busied with the cares of this World; find I shorten the time which I had appointed to Retirement and Self-examination, yet is this latter Exercise much needed: outwardly I may appear striving to perform my daily Duties well and circumspectly, but others know not the secret Faults of the Heart; the indolence, the imperfect Soul-lesse performances of Religious Duties: the obtruding of Selfish motives into what may seeme acts of Kindnesse or Charity. Often doth the verse of the 51st *Psalm* come to my remembrance, *Against Thee, Thee only have I sinned, and done this evil in Thy sight.* And now that I am a Mother it behoveth me still more to maintaine the Worke of inward Self-discipline. Even at my little Child's tender age, he is sensibly affected by the Feelings apparent in the faces of those around him: yesterday it happened as I nursed him, that being vexed by some trifling matters that were not done as I had desired, the disturbed expression of my Countenance so distressed him that he uttered a complaining Cry; made happy by a smile and the more serene aspect that affection called forth, he nestled his little Face again in my Bosom, and did soon fall asleep. It doth seeme a trifling thing to note, but it teacheth the Necessity of Watch-

1635.

July 7, Tuesday.

fulnesse; and if this Duty is especially called for in our Conduct towards the Young, or indeed towards all, is it not more so when we consider there is One who seeth the Heart, and whose eye will not behold iniquity?

Quiet Day, sitting the greater part thereof at my Embroidery; my *Mother* beside me knitting. We had much pleasant Converse: she encouraged me to persevere in the diligent performance of daily Duties whatsoever they may be; a good Wife, she sayd, should make it her chief desire to keep a well-order'd Family. My want of Experience, she kindly added, makes some things irksome and perplexing, which will cease to be the case after a while, when lesse time will suffice for their performance, and more opportunity afforded for rest of Body and Mind. She bade me not be cast down, or be discouraged by some mischances; and so comforted me. In the evening we paced for some time up and down the *Terrace*. The Moon arose above the old Oak Tree: my *Mother* seemed greatly to enjoy the Scene. I repeated aloud the 19th and part of the 92d *Psalmes*; and we entered the house: she looked chill, and I hastened to warm her some spiced Wine, which I took with a manchet of Bread for her Supper. As I gave Baby his laſt Meal for the night, my Heart was lifted up in Gratitude for the Mercy extended to me: he looked beautifull, & put his ſoft Hand to my Face careſſingly, his eyes full of Contentment and Affection looking into mine: May it ever be preſent with me, that this ſmall delicate Frame is the earthly Tabernacle of a Soul to be trained for Immortality.

Buſy in the *Still-Room* this forenoon: put the dried Roſe-leaves in paper bags. *Alice* was picking the Roſemary, and I ſat down to help her. She ſays the under Houſe-maid complains of ill treatment, particulars not worth writing of; her pretty Face gains too much of the good-will of the Men and the ill-will of the women: mentioned the Matter to the *Chaplain*, who ſaith he will add a few words of ſuitable exhortation at the concluſion of *Evening Service*. Bade *Alice* take heed there ſhould be a good ſtore of Chamomile-flowers and Poppy-heads, and of Mint water; our poore Neighbours look to us for ſuch: gave her my *Mother's* recipe for *Hungary* Water and the Conſerve of Hips.

John took the Yarn to the Weaver's, and

1635.

July 15, *Wedneſday*.

1635.

brought back Flax, Spices, and Sugar. The Stage Waggon had not arrived when he left *Ipswich*, and there was no package from *London*. My *Lord* was to send Hangings for the large Drawing Room; but it matters not.

July 18, Saturday.

A Day of many small Vexations, no sooner one mended than another appeareth: wearied Body and Mind, and yet I would humbly trust my Spirit was more quiet under the same than sometimes hath beene the case: no Letter or Message from my *Husband*.

Tried to collect my thoughts for Reading and Devotion, once strongly tempted to omit both, under the plea of Wearinesse and Unfitnesse, but resisted: read the 10th chapter of *St. Luke*, *Martha*, *Martha*, &c.: acknowledged and bewailed my Weaknesse. The sight of the young Face in the Cradle sent me to bed gratefull and happy.

August 3, Monday.

The last day of my *Mother's* Sojourn: tomorrow she setts forth into *Rutlandshire;* and there will remaine some Weeks before she returns to *Wimbledon*. My Lord *Noel* hath engaged to meet her at *Huntingdon*. May I be sensible of the greate Comfort and Happinesse in that I have been favoured to have my deare *Mother* so long with me: many sweet seasons

Lady Willoughby.

of quiet Meditation, and affectionate Intercourse have been vouchsafed: Words expressive of her owne humble and stedfast Faith, of Thankesgiving and Praise, fell from her Lippes; and precious Counsell and kind Incouragement to mee: to-night as I knelt before her, my Infant in my Arms, she laid her Hand upon my Head, and stroking it fondly said: Deare Child, may that little one be a Crown of rejoycing to thee as thou art to me; lead him early to *God*, my Daughter; to the *God* who has given him unto thee. Deare *Mother!*

Early in the fore-noon my honoured and deare *Mother* took her Departure: Let me think more of meeting againe than of the present payne of Parting. Some lines of *Ben Jonson* I do remember are swetely written to this effecte, they were given me by a young Friend at parting, who I beleeve was lesse indifferent towardes me, than I to him:

> *That Love's a bitter sweet I ne'er conceive*
> *Till the sower Minute comes of taking leave,*
> *And then I taste it: But as men drinke up*
> *In haft the bottom of a medicin'd Cup,*
> *And take some sirrup after, so doe I*
> *To put all relish from my Memorie*

1635.

August 4, Tuesday.

1635.

Of parting, drowne it in the hope to meet Shortly againe; and make our Abfence fweet.

Beloved *Mother*, the loffe of her prefence maketh my home lonely: but I have Work to doe, and ill fhould I fhow my Love for her, if it remaine neglected.

Aug. 17, Monday.

Rofe before fix: fought the Bleffing of the *Lord* upon my daily Path; read the 51 chap. *Ifaiah*, and 2d. St. *Luke*. Baby well: *John Armftrong* requefted to fee me concerning the Harveft-fupper. My *Lord* ftill abfent putteth me to much Trouble: the Harveft is nearly got in, only the Home-field remaines to be carted: *Armftrong* will take care enough as to the Supper; but the People will be difappointed unleffe I can prevail on *William Willoughby* to take his Brother's Place; hee ftands high in favour with our Neighbours, and the fame with our owne People; and if he could bring with him his young Kinsfolk, wee fhould not faile of Merriment.

Walked down to the Keeper's Lodge: Old *Bridget* fuffers from the rhewmatickes; bid her fend to the *Hall* for a Plaifter and fome Flannel; did my endeavours to perfuade her that the fame would bee of greater fervice than

Lady Willoughby.

the Charm given her by Dame *Stitchley;* though as fhe would not confent to leave it off, doubtleffe it will gaine all the credit, fhould *Bridget's* aches and paynes feem to amend. As I returned faw Horfemen coming up the *Avenue,* made fuch hafte as I could: Tydings of my deare *Lord;* but hee knows not when he can fett his face Home-wards; defireth mee to write by thefe Meffengers: they did ftay only to reft their Horfes. He fpeaks much in his Letter of a Painter named *Vandyck,* who ftands in great Favour at Court. The *King,* the *Princes,* and the Princeffe *Mary* have fat to him: The Ladies crowd to his Painting-room defirous to fee themfelves perpetuated by his gracefull Pencil.

The *Steward* from *Stixwood*-manor hath arrived: my *Lord* is much wanted to vifit his Eftates in *Lincolnfhire;* and Mr. *Legh* has bufineffe of various forts to fettle before *Michaelmafs-day:* but by none is he fo greatly defired as by his faithfull and loving Wife. My Inexperience makes the prefent Charge burthenfome, and I ever fear doing wrong, or omitting that which fhould bee attended to.

Baby grows finely, and fheweth already a mafterfull Spirit; he provides Work for my

1635.

Aug. 29, Saturday.

Needle, now the time is come that he fhould bee fhort-coated.

Arofe this Morning rejoycing in the hope that before the day clofed my deareft *Lord* would be fafely returned: the Day feemed long, but I had at laft the comfort of feeing him who is poffeffor of my Heart's trueft Affection arrive in health. He thought little *Billy* much improved: how happy were we in our quiet Home: furely the *lines have fallen to me in pleafant Places.*

Nov. 24, Tuefday.

The heavy Raine of late hath made much ficknefſe. to abound. Through mercy our Family are preferved in Health; and *Baby* has cut a Tooth, difcovered this morning by the fpoon knocking againſt it.

One *Thomas Parr* is dead at a wonderfull greate age, being, it is faid, 150 yeares old. The Earle of *Arundell* had him brought to *Whitehall,* and the change did fhortly affect his Health: no marvel, poore old Man, he would have beene better pleafed, methinks, to have beene lett alone.

Lady Willoughby.

1635-6.

THe *Hollanders* have sent an Embassy and a noble Present on the occasion of the *Queene* having another Daughter: there are rare pieces of China and Paintings, one by *Tytian*.

There is talk of a By-poste from *Wickham*, to join the North Poste, which is expected to run night and day betweene *Edinburgh* and *London*, to go thither and come back againe in six days: Men and Horses will scarce be found to doe this.

Young Mr. *Gage* is put into the *Bastille*. The Earle of *Leycester* hath kindly written to his Mother; he being Ambassador at this time she did apply to him for help in this troublous Affaire.

Baby walked a few steppes alone, and did

1635-6.

January.

Feb. 23, *Tuesday.*

June 6, *Monday.*

1636.

seem greatly pleased thereat, as were his Parents.

These Lines repeated by one at supper-time, who hath met with divers Mischances in his life:

> *The Fortunate have whole Yeares,*
>   *And those they chose:*
> *But the Unfortunate have onely Dayes,*
>   *And those they lose.*

Sept. 2, Friday.

At Dinner near twenty People; some remaine till next week; young *Harry-Vane*, the Lord *Brooke*, and others. My *Husband* brought me a Muff, and a Fan of Ostrichfeathers, and Sir *Philip Sydney's Arcadia:* the latter most suited to my taste; it is said the *King* dothe hold this Worke in high esteeme.

Sept. 6, Tuesday.

In looking back upon the last few dayes, I have to confesse in deep Humiliation of Spirit, that I have beene led away by a foolish vanitie, to take too much Pleasure in the Admiration of others, unworthy the Dignity of a Wife or a Mother: truly it is sayd *the Heart is deceitfull above all things, and desperately wicked.* For such share of Comelinesse as the *Creator's* Hand hath bestowed upon me, I would not that I should find therein food for Pride, or

Lady Willoughby.

Selfe-fatisfaction, beyond that it had found Favour in my *Lord's* Eyes, he who hath taken me to his Heart's true and pure Affection. I am his in all true Loyalty of Affection, and he doubteth not my Heart's Purity; but methought a fhade of Regret paff'd over his noble Countenance, as he beheld the Wife whom hee delighted to love and to honour, fo carried away by trifling and vanitie. And lett me not, in this Self-examination and fearching of my inmoft Heart, feek to hide from myfelfe that when he bade me *good night* at the Doore of my Clofet, inftead of lingering at my fide, as is his wont, a feeling of Refentment arofe, and as I enter'd and clofed the Doore, thoughts of Self-juftification prefented themfelves: but Confcience prevailed, and placed my Conduct in its true light: Selfe-reproach is hard to beare; not long fince, and I did think no Trial as regards others foe great as to meet with Injuftice, but to be the caufe of grieving another's Affection, and to feel lower'd in the Efteeme of one who hath beene ever readye to think more highly of me than I deferve; this is grievous to mee, and maketh me feeme hatefull in my owne eyes. I humbled myfelfe before the *Lord,* and pray'd that I might be-

1636.

come more watchfull, and ſtrive daily to follow the Example of *Him* who was meeke and lowly of Hearte.

Beloved *Huſband*, thy generous Love will forgive thy poore humbled Wife, who does in truth love thee, and reverence thy goodneſſe.

Sept. 8, Thurſday.

Let me not permit the Circumſtances of the laſt few days to paſſe from my Remembrance untill the Fault committed, and the Sorrow ariſing therefrom, have duly impreſſ'd my Mind: 1ſt, In the clearer inſight into this weake point of my Character, may I henceforth take more heed to my Ways: and 2ndly, with the Perception of how ſlight are the beginnings of Evill, as my deare *Mother* faith, if the Deſire of Praiſe take poſſeſſion of the Hearte, it becometh inſatiable, and doth eat away the root of all noble and generous Feeling; and even in leſſe degree gives a feveriſh reſtleſſ-neſſe, that leaves not the Mind and Affections free to ſpring up in ſtrength and beauty, ſeeking onely the Happineſſe of others. My deare *Huſband's* Gentleneſſe hath greatly endeared him to mee: may it be my conſtant Endeavour, by all dutifull Affection, to render myſelfe more worthy his Eſteeme and Love.

Sept. 17, Saturday.

After having paſſ'd a week in *Lincolnſhire*

Lady Willoughby.

wee are return'd Home. When at *Lincoln* my *Lord* tooke me to the *Cathedral*, and fhow'd mee the Tomb of his late Father, who died in that Citie in the yeare 1617. After him our little *Sonne* is named *William*: *Nurfe* fays *Baby* has not beene well for fome days paft, fhe thinks he is about his teeth.

Baby ill, reftleffe and feverifh, fent off a Meffenger to *Ipfwich* for the Phifitian there.

My poore Child worfe; he takes fcarce any nourifhment, and fuffers greate paine; he looks up fo piteoufly as if for help from thofe around him. The *Chaplaine* mentioned him by name at Prayers: this ftartled me: feeing others beleeve him fo ill, my feares encreafe.

No better to-day: I dare not think: Strength and Spirit needed to the utmoft; for he likes no one fo well to nurfe him, and hath ever a fweet Smile when I come againe after a fhort abfence. Oh *God*, fpare him to me: give mee not this bitter cup.

Weeks have paff'd and I am childleffe: yet doe I feeme as one not awaken'd from a frightfull dream. My Child, my Child.

The Fever hath left me weak: I dare not looke back, and there is nothing now left me to looke forward to. O *Mother*, my heart is

1636.

well nigh broken; how is it that I live? ſhall I ever be able to ſay, It is the *Lord*, lett him doe what ſeemeth unto him good. I thought to write downe ſome particulars of the Patience and Sweetneſſe, the Smile of Recognition when the parch'd Lipps could not ſpeake, but I cannot: he is out of payne, and I thank *God* for that.

Oct. 25, Tueſday.

Sat this morning for long with the *Bible* before me, thoughts too diſtracted to read; at laſt turn'd to the Hiſtory of the *Shunamite* woman; Alas! no Prophet was here to give me back my *Sonne*, and, alas! neither could I ſay unto the *Lord*, *It is well*, when he tooke from me his precious Gift. Beare with me, O mercifull *Father*: thou knoweſt the anguiſh of my Heart, and thou alone canſt enable me to ſay *Thy will, not mine, be done.*

My deare *Mother* writes to comfort me, but a ſorrow is now mine, in which even ſhe cannot give Comfort: She urgeth me to take care of my health for the ſake of others: but what is Life to me now? Yet will I try to beare in minde her Injunctions, though with a heavy Heart, and with more than indifference to the Proſpect before me. I turn away from the thought of looking upon another Infant's face;

all love for a Child is in the Grave: yet not in the Grave; it liveth in Heaven, my precious *Child*, with thy bleſſed Spirit: let me not ſpeak in bitterneſſe of a triall ſent me by the Almighty Hand.

 Oft times I ſeeme to have no power of giving my Mind to Prayer or Meditation, but walke about the houſe, or ſitt downe with a Booke or Needlework before me allmoſt without conſciouſneſſe & well-nigh without life. What doe all paſt Trialls & Vexations appeare, now a burthen of Sorrow is layd upon me, I am unable to beare? I had known Grief and Diſappointment, and already in my ſhort experience of life had learnt that this State of Exiſtence is onely a Preparation for Happineſſe hereafter, not Happineſſe itſelfe: But a precious *Gift* came from Heaven, my beautifull *Child* ſmil'd on me; I held it to my Heart, and did think it was my owne: What great evil have I done in thy ſight, O *God*, that thou haſt thus ſtricken me?

 At Prayers my *Lord* was ſenſibly affected by hearing the words *Suffer little Children to come unto me, and forbid them not: for of ſuch is the Kingdome of Heaven:* the beholding him thus over-come by ſtrong emotion led me to

1636.

Oct. 26, Wedneſday.

Oct. 27, Thurſday.

1636.

consider my owne Conduct, and I do feare me, I have beene very selfish in the Indulgence of my own Sorrow, too regardlesse of him who equally with me hath lost the deare *Sonne* of his Love, and who doth ever strive to strengthen and support me, and would fain lead me to take an Interest in our family Concerns, and in the Wellfare of our Neighbours, albeit Grief lieth heavy on his Heart. I felt another Reproof in his Looke of tendernesse and commiseration, as at our mid-day meal I sent away the plate the food untasted: I roused myselfe to exertion, and was repay'd the effort when his Eye rested on me approvingly. The Servants left the room, he took my Arm within his, and we walked to & fro in sweet and solemn Silence: my Heart, which had been strangely shut up, melted within me, when he utter'd a few gentle Words; and I felt there was yet something left to live for: Surely to him was due the poore remaining Powers of my Mind and Affections.

Oct. 29, Saturday.

Arose this morning with mind more composed than for some time past. *Cicely's* Mother ill, and I went down to see her: She is a bright Example of Patience, her Trialls and Sufferings have beene manifold, bodily pain the least, has lost three Children in infancy and one daughter grown up: and yet, can it be, has known ſtill deeper ſorrow.

Return'd through the *Park*: never ſaw the Cheſtnuts and Beeches more beautiful in their autumn tints, the fallen Leaves cruſhed pleaſantly beneath my Feet, the Sun was ſetting before I was aware, and the Aire grew ſuddenly chill. Taking the neareſt way, I entered the houſe by a ſide door, and there beneath the old Mulberry ſaw the little Cart and Whip as they had beene left by my poore Child the laſt day he was out, when he look'd ſo tired, and I carried him in. I ſtooped and took up the Whip, and hiding it beneath my cloke, went ſtraight up ſtairs: no Hand had touched it ſince his: the teares I wept over it did me good: it ſeemed my innocent right to weep over this Token of my *loſt one.*

Health and ſtrength mend: make a point of walking in the *Long Gallery* whenſoever the weather admits not of my going out: while ſo employed repeat Pſalms and other portions of *Holy Writ*, therein finding profitable Subjects of Meditation and peaceful Thoughts: Often has been brought to my Mind the Text *I was brought low, and he helped me:* now, is my deare *Mother's* Care repaid, in the Help I find

Nov. 14, Monday.

1636.

Nov. 15,
Tuesday.

it to have by me such recollection of the Lessons she taught.

My early Habits in the morning have been sadly interrupted: frequent restlesse nights, often sleeplesse for hours together, and awakening languid and ill at ease; often in the long nights my Fancy is disquieted in looking forward to again becoming a Mother, and that ere long, least haply the Infant nourished beneath a heart so saddened by Grief, should, if permitted to enter on existence, be deprived of that Joyfullnesse of nature which is the Birth-right of the young Spirit; but whatever may be in the Ordering of my *Heavenly Father*, let me submit: too often have I rebelled against his just Appointments. In the words of the *Psalmist* let me pray, *Enter not into judgement with thy Servant, O Lord, my Spirit is overwhelmed within me, my Heart within me is desolate: hide not thy Face from me: in thee do I trust.*

1636-7.

Nce more with a gratefull Heart, doe I record the Mercy of our *Heavenly Father*, in that he hath permitted his unworthy Servant to live to behold the Face of another *Little One*. Yet now muft I rejoyce with trembling over a Being fo fraile: the fulneffe and brightneffe of joy of a young Mother can never againe be my Experience, fince that joy has bene the Source of a Suffering and Agony never to be forgotten. Death follow'd into the Habitation wherein Life had juft tooke up its abode. Not in fhort fpace of time can the Heart recover fuch Difpenfations, and in the Excellency of no after joys can it ever forget the ftroke that firft deftroyed its fweeteft Hopes: Death once feene at our hearth leaveth a Shaddow which abideth there for ever. During

1636-7.

the long period of Sickneſſe that has beene my portion, I have endeavour'd through the *Divine Grace*, profitably to employ the ſolitary Houres, and doe now ſee much Mercy in the return to Health being graduall. The needfull Quiett led me to ſeek a Spirituall Communion, whereby I humbly hope I am the better fitted for the Performance of the ſeveral Duties of Life, truſting not in my owne Strength, that truly would be a broken reed. *Lord! thy rod and thy ſtaff they comfort me:* yea, even the rod, though it hath ſmitten me to the earth.

January 13, Friday.

The *Chriſtening* is to be next weeke: the name, after ſome difficulty in deciding thereon, fixed to be *Diana*. But few of our Relations are aſked this time to be preſent; to both of us the ceremony will give riſe to melancholly thought. Overheard *Nurſe* telling one of the Women that at the former *Chriſtening* the Infant cried not: there is a Country Saying, that a Child which crieth not when ſprinkled in *Baptiſm* will not live.

1637. May Day.

We walked down to the *Village* at an early houre, juſt in time to ſee the Proceſſion of the May-pole, which was adorned with Ribbons and Garlands: Lads and Laſſes were at their merry Games, the Queene, in her holie-day

Lady Willoughby.

Finery and Crowne of floures, looking happier than the Wearer of a real Crown, I ween: groups of Old People looking on: for a while there was a lack of Young Men and Maidens: but a number fhortly appeared as *Robin Hood, Maid Marien, &c.* Methought fome of the Elder Folks look'd grave, and at one fide of the Green a ftern looking Man, dreff'd in a loofe Coat, and a high crown'd hat, with the hair cut clofe, had collected a good many round him, and was holding forth in a loud harfh tone. My *Hufband* left me and went towards them: after liftening a few minutes to the Difcourfe, he made as though he would fpeak; but mett with difcourteous reception, and return'd with a fmile on his face, faying, The Speaker look'd on his long curl'd Locks, and lace Ruffs with too great Abhorrence to think him worthy his Notice, and onely went on with the more Bitterneffe to fet forth the diabolical Wickedneffe of the Dance and the Vanity of all fuch Amufements. I fate mee down by old *Bridget,* who had hobbled down in fpite of her reumaticke paynes: poore *Smythe* too had crept out, wan and feeble from ague. After a while, the fport feeming to flag, my *Lord* offer'd to head a party at *Prifon-bars,* and was cordially greeted,

1637.

and *William Willoughby* coming up with a Sonne of Sir *Robert Crane* and one or two more young Men, the game was sett on with great spiritt. Ale and Victuals came down from the *Hall* and other Quarters, and I left the *Greene*. There was no want of Merriment the rest of the day: and the Preacher and his Party remained not long to interfere with the usuall Proceedings.

June 1,
Thursday.

The deare Child thrives apace: againe and againe I looke at her in the Cradle & say, *Lord, spare this one unto me.* I have thought myselfe resigned to my Losse; howbeit, a Weight is on my Spiritt that no Effort or Time has yet shaken off: will it be ever thus? Young as I am, is Hope so blighted that it will never more unfold its faire Blossom? Let me not indulge these Meditations: but be willing to take up my *Crosse* dayly, and follow after *Christ*. He hath promised to make the Burthen light to such as come to him.

June 27.
Tuesday.

Hope that I have latterly made some Progresse in the subduing Selfe, so far as attaining unto a greater Desire to give up my own will to that of others, and conform to their pleasure; more especially his who hath rightfull Claim to my dutifull Obedience and Companionship in thofe matters that intereft him: herein onely can true Satisfaction be found in wedded Life: may I every day more and more feeke to find Satisfaction and Pleafure in thofe Things wherein he is concerned. At noon to-day we walk'd down to the Sheep-Shearing: the poor Sheep ftruggle at the firft againft their fate, but how quietly do they fubmit in the end: the Lambs did keep up a continued Bleating; it is a marvell how they find out their owne Mothers, who come back to them fo changed. One large Ram butted with fuch force againft one of the younger Lads that he pufh'd him into the Water: much laughter thereat, and many a paffing Joke we heard on his overthrow. On our way home two curley-headed Children prefented us with Pofies of Gilliflowers and Cowflip tufts, of which they had their aprons full: bade them go up to the *Hall* with them: we gave them a Silver Groat, which they look'd at with fome perplexity, but curtfied & thank'd us with truftfull Countenances: the youngeft one, ftrong made and active, look'd not much older than our fweet Child might have now bene, had he lived.

Late in the day Mr. *Gage* rode up: he tells us Mr. *John Hampden* hath refufed the late

1637.

demand for Ship-money: Discontent increasing every where. The proceedings of the *Starre Chamber* against *Prynne* and others have roused the whole country, even many who before tooke not part with the Malcontents doe now expresse their Abhorrence of this Tyranny. My *Husband* will go to *London* straightway.

July 24, Monday.

With a heavy heart saw my deare *Lord* depart this forenoon: *Armstrong* accompanying him as farr as *Ipswich*: Struggled against desponding Thoughts, and pass'd some time in the *Nursery*, to give myselfe Occupation of Mind as well as Hands. After a Walk on the *Terrace*, went to *Alice's* Room: she hath long beene ailing: sate some while with her, to cheer her, as I knew she would take to heart this voyage to *London*, which Place, in her eyes, doth abound with all manner of Wickednesse and Danger.

July 25, Tuesday.

To-night *John Armstrong* returned, bearing me a kind Farewell from his Master. He sayth Mr. *John Hampden's* Refusal is greatly talked about: likewise it is rumour'd the Lord *Say* hath refused the Demand for Ship-money with equal pertinatiousnesse. *Armstrong* stopp'd as he pass'd through *Wickham* at the Blacksmith's, the Head-quarters of News and Country Gossip:

he there met with a Packman, who fays there be terrible Tumults in the North: at *Edenburgh* the *Bifhop* well nigh killed, Stones and other Miffiles thrown at him in the Pulpit, fo foon as he commenced reading the *Prayer Booke*, as ordered in *Council:* on leaving the Church he was caft down and nearly trod to death. Some fay the King is like to go to *Edenburgh* to fettle thefe matters in perfon with the *Prefbytery.*

Tidings of my *Lord:* he keeps well in health: he faith Judgement in Mr. *Hampden's* caufe is deferred till next Term: two of the Judges are on his fide.

Baby well: have fome Thoughts of weaning her, my own ftrength failing: but put it off day after day, it is hard to difmiffe her from the food and warmth which have been hers by right fo long, and break this firft Bond of Companionfhip and mutual Dependence.

From the Diary of

1638-9.

Date wanting.

1638-9.

Since Judgement hath beene given against Mr. *Hampden*, my deare *Husband* hath had divers Conferences with the Lords *Say* and *Brooke*, respecting their leaving the Country. One Mr. *Oliver Cromwell* they speak of, as much stirr'd by the unhappy state of Affaires, and they have found him to be a man of shrewd Judgement, and possessing great Energy and Determination.

The *King* at *Yorke*: and has required the Nobility and Officers to take an Oath that they do abhorr all Rebellions, and especially such as do arise out of Religion. The Lords *Say* and *Brooke* refusing to take the same, have been dismiss'd to their homes. The *King* proceedeth to *Berwick*, there to meet the *Scotch* Deputies.

Much Discontent that the *King* calleth no *Parliament*.

Lady Willoughby.

1639-40.

1639-40.
January 1,
Wednesday.

MY firſt thoughts are due to thee, O *Heavenly Father*, who haſt mercifully permitted the paſt Yeare to cloſe and the preſent to open upon us, a thankfull and happy Family: Graciouſly accept my imperfect Thankſgiving, and the Adoration of a Heart which I with unfeigned humility anew dedicate to thee. By the Aide of thy *Holy Spirit* lead me every day I live to love thee more worthily and ſerve thee more acceptably. May I truly repent of my manifold Tranſgreſſions, my Pride, my rebellious Spirit which hath too often ſtruggled againſt the juſt Appointments of thy Providence: do thou, O *God*, renew a right Spiritt within me. Lord, thou haſt made mee to be a Mother, O yet ſpare the ſweet *Children* thou haſt given unto me: and may I never loſe ſight of the Duty which is entruſted to me;

1639-40.

but so train them that they may be all gathered into thy Fold, at the greate Day of Account. May thy Blessing rest upon them, upon my *Husband*, and on all deare unto us. And to thy fatherly Care, thy Wisdom, and thy Love may we trust all that concerns us, in unshaken Faith, and in the blessed Hope of eternal Life, through *Jesus Christ* our *Lord* and *Saviour*.

Went to the *Nurserie:* little *Fanny* yet asleep. Took *Di* by the hand, and went down to Prayers: she was very quiet and well-behaved, and as she knelt down betweene her Father and me, my Mind was brought into a state of much Sweetnesse and Repose as the gracious Invitation of the blessed *Saviour* to bring our little Children unto him, was brought to my remembrance.

Methought the *Chaplain's* Discourse favour'd somewhat of pharisaical gloom and austerity, and we were therefore in no little perplexity when *Armstrong* came into the *Hall* after breakfast, to say the Domestics petition'd for a Dance and *Christmasse* Games to-night according to old Usage. We gave our consent. The *Chaplain* expressed his Dissatisfaction, neverthelesse the Evening past merrily: a goodly

Assembly were gather'd together of our Neighbours, and to show our Good-will we looked on for a while, and my *Lord* led off the firste Dance with the Bailiff's Daughter: the young Men of our Party followed his Example, and chose out the prettiest looking Damsels, my favourite *Cicely* being one of them; and they went down a long Country Dance, well pleased therewith. Old blind *John* and his Son play'd the viol and pipe: Games followed, bob-apple and the like: and *Alice* had taken good care for the Supper. Sounds of Laughing and Singing reached us long after we left them.

 Newes hath reached us that the *King* has dissolved the *Parliament* though so lately mett, he being offended by the *Commons* passing a Resolution that the Discussion and Redresse of Grievances should precede the Vote of Supply. They complained that the interference of the *Lords* was a Violation of their Priviledges. An eloquent Speech by Mr. *Waller:* such a House suited not the *King*.

 My *Husband* writes me word that Mr. *Bellasis* and Sir *John Hotham* are sent to the *Tower*, onely Offence alleged, their Speeches. The House of the Lord *Brooke* searched for Papers, his Study and Cabinets broken open. A Con-

1640.

May 7,
Thursday.

May 9,
Saturday.

1640.

vocation of Clergy hath bene held, the Canons iſſued by them, ſuch as to throw the whole Nation into a ferment. Writs of Ship-money in greater number than ever, and Bullion ſeized, the property of Merchants, and kept by them in the *Tower* for Safety.

May 25, Monday.

No News for ſome days. The Chapter of the Morning greatly impreſſ'd my Mind with the Goodneſſe of *God* towards his feeble and ignorant Children: the *Holy Scriptures* do abound with Words of Conſolation and Encouragement to the poore and lowly, *the hewers of wood and drawers of water: the meek will he guide in judgement.* Learning and great Ability, bleſſed be *God*, are not needed to the right Underſtanding of the Good Tydings of the *Goſpel.*

The poore blind Widow pondering in her Heart the Words of *Jeſus*, her Memory ſtored with the Readings of her younger days, her Spirit rich in Love and Faith, findeth the true Bread of Life, and is perhaps more capable of receiving the Enlightening of the *Holy Spirit* in the Study of Divine Truth, than the Learned who truſt in their own reaſon and ſcholaſtick attainements. Alſo in looking for what is *God's* Will concerning them, I oft think the poore simple minded People have a wife Judgement given to them in the Businesse of Life. A Visit to old *Betty's* Cottage seldom faileth to give me such Sense of her truely virtuous and pious Life, as to make me look upon this paterne of Goodnesse with sincere desire to follow the same. She hath lost Husband and Children, save one Son onely who left her years agoe: she knoweth not if he be yet living: and she hath been totally blind more than fifteen yeares. Truely hath Patience here her perfect work.

 The *Mayor* and *Sheriffe* of *London* have beene brought before the *Starre Chamber* for Slacknesse in Levying the Ship-mony. May 27, *Wednesday.*

 Both Children ill the past week: through Mercy recovering. Little *Fanny* but just saved: my onely Experience in a child's illnesse having beene so unhappy, I found it hard to keep my feares in subjection; yet was it very needfull. What shall I render unto the *Lord* for all his benefits? June 17, *Wednesday.*

 Have much comfort in the serious and feeling way in which little *Di* says her Prayers: she is too young to understand much, but the Habit is important, and wee know not at how earlye an age the *Holy Spirit* communeth with

1640.

1640.

the tender Heart of the young. And a Child's Mind ſtops not at Difficulties as ours does: when told that *God* heareth Prayer from his Throne in Heaven, the belief is entire, and ſhe queſtioneth not. I verily believe, the Doctrine that we ſhould walk by Faith and not by Sight, is eaſier to a young Child than to us, whoſe Affections have become engrafted on earthly Objects, and the firſt Simplicity of Faith obſcured. And ſurely we ſhould conſider it a ſacred Truſt given to us, to direct this in-born Truſt and ready Belief of the little Child to *Him* who implanted it.

June 27, Saturday.

Nurſerie proſpers: *Di* vaſtly ſtronger, and hungry as *Nurſe* can deſire. *Fanny's* Cheeks too are ſomewhat more plump and roſy.

July 24, Friday.

The young Prince hath beene chriſten'd Henry, the ceremonie perform'd at Oatlands by the Archbiſhop of Canterbury.

Sept. 1, Tueſday.

The Birth of this my third Baby now living, occaſion of renewed Thankſgiving and Praiſe: though I doubt not duly thankful, yet my deare *Huſband* had hoped another Sonne would have beene given him; and this proving otherwiſe, hath brought ſome Diſappointment. He would have counted it a great Happineſſe to have ſeene an Heir to his Title and Eſtates:

but he fayeth not much on the fubject, and methought kiffed his new-borne *Daughter* with a gladfome Smile upon his Countenance. I had the wifh fhe fhould be named *Theodofia*, after my deare and honour'd *Mother*: but my *Lord* did fo greatly defire that fhe fhould be called *Elizabeth*, after mee, I confented thereto, wifhing to confult his Pleafure in this, as in all things elfe in which it can be confulted by any giving up on my parte: though I the more regret that it muft be fo, feeing that my Uncle *Noel* has not given the Name of *Theodofia* to either of his Daughters.

Find myfelfe unable to attend much to houfehold Affaires, and leave them to *Alice's* faithfull overfight.

Lord *Say* writes that a Petition has beene prefented to the *King* by twelve *Peers*, praying him to call a *Parliament*; fo likewife have the Citizens of *London*.

Meffenger arrived from the Mayor of *Ipfwich*: Writts are iffued for the 3rd of *November*. It is hoped Mr. *Oliver Cromwell* will be return'd for *Cambridge*. My deare *Hufband* hath again departed: he doth hope to return for a few Days at *Chriftmaffe*.

The *King* hath opened *Parliament* in perfon:

1640.

Sept. 26, Saturday.

Oct. 20, Tuefday.

1640.
Nov. 9,
Monday.

they ſay he look'd pale and dejected. The *Commons* did make Choice in haſte of *Lenthall* a Barriſter for *Speaker*, inſtead of one *Gardiner*, he being the *King's* Choice. They have paſſ'd a Reſolution that *Prynne*, *Burton*, and Dr. *Baſtwick* ſhould be ſent for forthwith by Warrant of the Houſe. The Table is loaded with Petitions, preſented by hundreds crying out *No Biſhops: No Starre Chamber*.

Dec. 2,
Wedneſday.

On the 28th the three *Puritans*, as they are called, liberated from their diſtant Dungeons, came up to *London*, and were mett by 5000 Perſons.

Dec. 15,
Tueſday.

Heard to-day that the Earle of *Strafford* was committed to the *Tower*. It is ſayd he urgently declined appearing in the *Houſe*, but the *King* inſiſted, making him ſolemn Aſſurances of Safety: but he no ſooner enter'd the *Houſe* than he was put under Arreſt.

Dec. 24,
Thurſday.

The determined Meaſures of the *Commons* fill all People with Amazement. The *Archbiſhop* of *Canterbury* is accuſed of High Treaſon, and committed to the *Uſher*: it is ſayd he hath beene forced to ſell his plate to raiſe money wherewith to pay the fine of 500 pounds. And a Reſolution has been paſſ'd, that for *Biſhops* or other *Clergymen* to be in the Commiffion of the Peace, or to have any Judicial Powers in the *Starre Chamber*, or in any Civil Courts, is a hindrance to their Spiritual Functions, &c. This feemeth true enough: greate need have all Parties to pray to be preferved from Exceffe, or being carried away by the heate of Party Spirit and perfonal Refentment. The Cruelty and Severity exercifed by Archbifhop *Laud* in *Scotland*, and the Earl's Tyranny and Wickedneffe in *Ireland*, have raifed them enemies, who wifh nothing fo much as their Death.

From the Diary of

1640-1.

After Prayers this morning my *Lord* beckoned to the Servants to remaine: He commended them for the faithfull performance of their Duties, and expreſſed his Confidence in their ſteady Attachment and Services, eſpecially in his abſence, which was like to be protracted: They bowed and curtſied; and *Armſtrong*, as Spokeſman for the reſt, ſayd, You may depend upon us all, my Lord: our Hearts and our Hands are my Lady's, *God* bleſſe her.

I knew not till to-day that my *Huſband's* Return would be more uncertaine than hath often beene the caſe: it dependeth much upon the Termination of Lord *Strafford's* Tryal: moſt are of the minde he will be found guilty; & that nothing can then ſave him, unleſſe the *King* prove that he can be true to his promiſe,

when the Life of one whom he hath ever pro-
fess'd to hold in great Esteeme and Affection,
is at stake: but no man trusts the *King*. The
better ground of hope for *Strafford*, is the
lenient Temper of the good Earl of *Bedford*,
and his Influence with the *House*.

In the forenoon accompanied my *Husband*
at the Settlement of Accounts with *Armstrong*:
and assisted in copying the different Items into
the Booke wherein my *Lord* hath entered for
some yeares past the Items of Personal and
Family Charges; keeping another for the
Accounts of Income, Rents, &c. chiefly from
his *Lincolnshire* Property; this Manor bringing in but little.

This was new Worke to mee; but I did
my best, it seeming desirable I should, so
farre as my poore Ability serveth, render myselfe competent to settle Accompts with *Armstrong* every weeke, as is the practice of my
Lord when he is at Home: and likewise he
wisheth mee to be acquainted with our Re-
sources. He had wonderfull Patience with
my Ignorance, and did kindly commend my
unskillfull Performance, not suffering me to
be discouraged, though I proved more Hindrance than Help. I had had so many Feares

1640-1.

both of doing wrong and incurring his Displeasure, that in my Satisfaction I kissed the deare Hand that did with so much ease correct my Errors, gratefull to the kind Heart by which it was guided.

January 11, Monday.

Sir *John Hotham* arrived from *Hull* on his way to *London:* and purposing to proceed to-morrow, my deare *Lord* will accompany him. Sir *John* seemeth well disposed. Thought my *Husband* gave much Heed to his Conversation, as he remarked that with twelve Men, Arms, and Provision, he could hold out this House against a considerable Force, and went into the Detail of the Arrangements he would make, if it so chanced it was attacked by an Enemy.

These are fearefull times, let mee be encreasingly vigilant; and whatsoever happeneth, be faithfull to the Duties of my present Station, Wife and Mother; and a large Household, the Charge whereof is much left to mee: sufficient Care for one of but little Experience, and with Health not so good as might be wished.

January 12, Tuesday.

Read in *Isaiah* chapter 26, these Words of Comfort: *Thou keepest him in perfect Peace whose Mind is stayed upon Thee, because he trusteth in Thee:* May I attaine unto this trust, need have I of better Strength than my own at this Time when my dearest *Life* may be in circumstances of Danger; at a Time like this, who is safe? the *King* ever playing false with the *Commons*, and disregarding their Privileges, & the *House* now sitting in Judgement on his favoured Servant: yet whatsoever Danger may threaten, I would not that my *Husband* should desert his Poste; rather let mee rejoyce that he standeth up in his place to defend the People's Rights. My two Cousins from *Rutlandshire* will beare me company during some Portion of his Absence. What Mercy that our little Ones are well, and that I am not left in a childlesse Home.

1640-1.

On Monday the *Archbishop* was removed to the *Tower* from Master *Maxwell's* house where he hath beene allowed to remaine since his commitment: from *Cheapside* to the *Tower* he was followed and railed at by the people, the which he took quietly.

March 6, Saturday.

Turning back the leaves of this *Diary* I see many Interruptions, in some Places for Months together, no Notice or Note of any sort. The Period of my deare *Mother's* last Sicknesse is unrecorded: but so deeply engraven on my Memory are the Events of that mournfull Time, that I believe I may without danger of

March 8, Monday.

1640-1.

Error therein, commit to Paper some few Particulars. It may be a Satisfaction hereafter, that these should not be trusted wholly to Recollection, which may then fail me.

I remember as clearly as if 'twas no longer ago than yesterday, the Day whereon my *Mother* arrived, which did afterwards prove to be the last time it was ever my Happinesse to welcome her under our Roof. The Afternoon was calm and beautifull, and the Sunne low in the West caused the Shadows to fall at length acrosse the Grasse, the Honeysuckle over the Doorway was covered with its pale luscious Flowers, which hung down untill some of the trailing Branches lost themselves in the old Sweet-brier Bush, and the White Rose, my *Mother's* favourite Tree, was arrayed in its faire Blossoms. As we stood looking at these, she did presently arrive. Methought she stepped feebly from her Coach; and when I gave her such aid as I could, she sayd with a mournfull yet sweet smile, I need a stronger Arme now than thine, my *Daughter:* one equally kind, I do fully believe, she added as she leaned on my *Husband's*. Saddest Thoughts took hold of me, yet did I use my best endeavour to conceal the Feare that struck suddenly on my Heart, that her Tarryance here would not be for long. She looked better when feated in her accuftomed Chaire: and her pale Cheek had a delicate colour, which gave me a Hope that her Weakneffe was not fo great as at firft did appeare, and that the Difficulty in Walking might be from her having fate fo long in the Coach, caufing a degree of Stiffneffe. Before retiring to her Chamber, fhe had converfed with much of her ufuall Chearfulneffe: wee accompanied her up the ftaires one on each fide of her: when taking leave for the night, fhe faid to my *Hufband*, I feare me I fhall be a Burthen to you, Lord *Willoughby*, but not for long: but I meant not your kind Heart would fo confider me. I thank you; thank you both: may God bleffe you.

For the fpace of two or three weekes my *Mother's* State did fo alternate day by day, the one day feeming to regaine the Strength loft the previous one, that I perceived not any great Change in her Appearance, fave that her Breathing was fomewhat hurried by any exertion more than common. I read to her daily, morning and evening Portions of the *Scriptures*, her favourite Paffages often repeated: of fuch I might make particular Mention, of the *Pfalmes* and the

1640-1.

Gospells. She did frequently remark thereon with much earnestnesse and sweetnesse. She was able most days to walk out a little: and sometimes, she, being unwilling to disappoint my Desires, would consent to be borne on a Chaire by two of the Men, never failing to thank them with much Kindnesse of manner, and expressing her concerne at giving this Trouble. One fore-noon I did prevaile with her to let them carry her a considerable distance from the House, to a sheltered sunny Spot, whereunto we did oft resort formerly to hear the Wood-pigeons which frequented the Firre Trees hereabout. We seated ourselves, and did passe an houre or two very pleasantly: she remarked how mercifully it was ordered, that these Pleasures should remaine to the last Days of Life; that when the Infirmities of Age make the Company of others burthensome to us, and ourselves a burthen to them, the quiet Contemplation of the Workes of *God* affords a simple Pleasure which needeth not aught else than a contented Minde to enjoy: the Singing of Birds, even a single Flower, or a pretty Spot like this, with its bank of Primroses and the Brooke running in there below, and this warm Sunshine, how pleasant are they. They take back the Thoughts to our Youth, which Age doth love to look back upon. She then related to me many Paſſages of her early Life, wherein was obſervable the ſame Love of natural Beauty that doth now miniſter in ſo large a meaſure to our Enjoyment.

The ſweet Seaſon of Spring was delightfull to her beyond any other Time of the Yeare: yet in all did ſhe recognize the bountifull Hand of the *Creator:* and moſt aptly drew from all his Workes thoſe Divine Teachings made manifeſt to the pious and lowly Minde unto whom *Day unto Day uttereth Speech, and Night unto Night ſheweth Knowledge.* In the Quietneſſe of Contemplation, the ſtill ſmall voice of *God* findeth a Place in the Heart : ſhe had liſtened thereunto in the days of her Youth, and in Age ſhe reapeth her Reward : the Yeares draw not nigh unto her when ſhe will ſay *I have no pleaſure in them.* Such were my thoughts, as I beheld her placid Enjoyment, and heard her commend the delicate Beauty of a Flower ſhe held in her Hand, remarking that ſhe look'd upon this Portion of Creation as in a particular manner worthy of our ſacred regard, the Flowers of the Field being ſanctified by our *Lord* teaching from them Leſſons of Faithfulneſſe in the

1640-1.

Wifdom and Love of our *Heavenly Father*. She afked me if I would repeate the 90th and 91ft *Pfalmes*, which I did for the moft part; fhe repeated after me the words, *Yet is their Strength Labour and Sorrow*. Three fcore and ten Yeares I have not feene: and this lengthened Span of Life may not be ordained for me, yet in the latter Days of my Pilgrimage thus farre toward the Grave, the *Lord* hath layd upon me no Burthen which his Love hath not made light and eafy to be borne: Sight and Hearing remaine, and the Ufe of my Limbs fo farre as an old woman needeth. Surely Goodneffe and Mercy have followed me all the Days of my Life, and will, I doubt not, to the clofe: and my evening Sun will, I humbly hope, be permitted to fet in brightneffe. She took a Rofebud which I had gathered, and fayd, This bud will never open; but fome there are which will unfold in Heaven. She look'd earneftly in my Face: I perceived her meaning, My precious *Child*, mine that is in Heaven, I fayd, and could not refraine from Teares. Calm thyfelfe, my *Daughter*: I fhall foone meet him, if I am found worthy to be where his pure Spirit is: let me feel as a Link between thy Soul and his. Oh that I may one day meet there all my deare

Lady Willoughby.

1640-1.

Children: many have been my Bereavements, but Mercy, tender Mercy was in all my Afflictions. We arofe, and fhe was able to walk a good part of the Way towards the Houfe, untill the Servants mett us. Henceforth my *Mother* left the Houfe but feldom, and foone fhowed herfelf incapable of this much exertion: her ftrength diminifhed daily, and fhe became fcarce able to quit her chamber.

She defired one day to fpeak with my *Hufband*, and communicated to him her conviction that there remained to her but a fhort Time to live, and requefted him to prepare me for her immediate departure to *Wimbledon*, talking of fetting forth the next Day: but it was too late, fhe was too weake to bear moving: fhe tooke to her bed, and I thenceforth left her not, fave when wanted in the *Nurferie*.

One Night, it was the *Sabbath*, fhe called us both to her Bed-fide, expreffed her Happineffe in beholding us fo united in the bonds of Affection and Friendfhip: in a moft touching manner addreffed my *Hufband*, commended me as her chief earthly Treafure to his continued tender Care and Love, and then, the Teares running down her Face, thanked him for the Kindneffe and Gentleneffe he had alwayes fhewn to her beloved *Daughter*: she pressed our two Hands together, rays'd herselfe up, and in a low tremulous Tone, slowly utter'd as nearly as I can remember them, these Words:

Allmighty Father, *behold these my Children: blesse them in each other and in their Children: keepe them in the Path of Righteousnesse: protect them in Danger, comfort them in Affliction, and when they come to passe through the Valley of the Shadow of Death, let their spirit faint not, neither be afraid: but let them lay hold on the Promises of Eternal Life, through Faith in* Christ Jesus *our* Lord *and* Saviour. Amen.

She sunk back exhausted, and revived not againe to hold much Intercourse with us. Her Countenance, though at times marked by Suffering, was Calm and Peacefull: her Eyes mostly closed as in Sleep: the Silvery Hair parted on her Forehead: she lay throughout the remainder of the day without taking notice of any thing: twice or thrice she ask'd for Water to drink, and smil'd affectionately upon all around.

Late in the evening she sayd, Is *Mabel* here? her faithfull Servant approach'd near the Bed. She had taken leave the day before of such of our Domestics as she knew personally, and now gave Messages of Remembrance to those at *Wimbledon*, not forgetting one or two poore aged Woemen to whom she had beene a good Friend in their old Age of Poverty. Againe she became much exhausted, and we thought the faint Breathing must soon cease: but she so remained some houres. About five of the clock in the morning she opened her eyes: the early Sunne shon in at the Casement, which was at the farthest side from the Bed: she appeared conscious of the Daylight, and we could partly distinguish the Words, *Heaven, no Sun, the Glory of God, the light thereof*. She look'd on all that were neare unto her, and we thought she sayd, *Deare Children*. I stoop'd to kisse her: with a last Effort she returned my Embrace; and as I gently layd her Head on the Pillow, her pure Spirit left its earthly Mansion.

In the stillnesse of this awful Moment, my Mind was impress'd with the Belief that her passing Spirit look'd on her weeping Family with a Love set free from all earthly Feare in the perfect Fruition of Faith, which was become her blessed Experience, knowing that our Sorrow would be but for a Mòment compared to the *eternal Weight of Glory*. Dearest *Mother*,

1640-1.

may thy precious Example be ever present with me. I felt it a sore Triall, the House being at this time full of Company, yet believe it might be good for me that there were so many to be cared for. My Sister *Dorothy* was truly kind: *Albinia* was prevented coming: My Lord *Noel* was a true Mourner, a more than common Affection united him in Bonds of Intimacy with his late Sister, and he sought every Opportunity of Converse with me, and pass'd much Time of every Day alone in her favourite Walks: his Daughter *Eleanor* had accompanied him out of *Leicestershire:* before he left us, my Deare Uncle had gained the Love and Esteeme of all.

I may here write an Inscription to the Memory of the late Mistresse *Hampden*, which my Lord did copy from her Tomb in the Church at *Great Hampden*, when he was last at that Place, the same appearing to me particularly suited to the Subject of the last pages of this *Diary*, wherein my Pen would faile, were I to attempt to describe her Excellence, or my own great Losse.

To the eternal Memory of the truely Vertuous and Pius *Elizabeth Hampden*, Wife of *John Hampden*, the tender Mother of an happy Offspring in 9 hopefull Children: In her Pilgrimage the Staie and Comfort of her Neighbours, the Love and Glory of a well-ordered Family, the Delight and Happineſſe of tender Parents, but a Crowne of Bleſſings to a Huſband: In a Wife, to all an eternal Paterne of Goodneſſe, and Cauſe of Joye whilſt ſhe was: In her diſſolution a Loſſe unvaluable to each, yet herſelfe bleſt, and they recompenſed, in her Tranſlation from a Tabernacle of Claye and fellowſhipp with Mortalls to a celeſtiall Manſion and Communion with *Deity*, The 20th Day of *Auguſt* 1634. *John Hampden*, her ſorrowfull Huſband, in perpetuall Teſtimony of his conjugal Love, hath dedicated this Monument.

My *Mother* in a ſpecial manner did walke by Faith. In all Trouble ſhe could ſay, It is good for me to be afflicted, it is the *Lord*, let him do what ſeemeth to him good: and in time of Proſperity and Gladneſſe ſhe forgot not the Giver of all Mercies, the Song of Thankſgiving and Prayſe was in her Heart and on her Lippes: Scrupulous in the exact Performance of all her Duties, ſhe regarded none as too inſignificant

1640-1.

to be done well: to the Poore fhe was a kind and bountifull Friend; and as *Hampden* fayth of his Wife, fhe was a Paterne of Goodneffe, and Caufe of Joy to all who knew her: and the *Lord* permitted his aged Servant to depart in Peace. Bleffed be his Name!

March 11, Thurfday.

This Morning arofe fomewhat earlier than ufuall, and felt the Benefit of fo doing throughout the day: Mind compofed and ftrengthened. At five of the Clock my Coufins *Anne* and *Margaret* arrived: feem warm-hearted young Women, *Anne* grown into more Comelineffe than fhe appeared likely to do, two yeares since: *Margaret* lovely as a bright Morning in May, the calme Truthfulneffe of her Countenance brings to mind *Spenfer's* Verfes to the Memorie of his beloved Friend,

> *A fweet attractive kind of Grace,*
> *A full Affurance given by Lookes,*
> *Continuall Comfort in a Face*
> *The Lineaments of* Gofpell *Bookes:*

the two laft Lines efcape my Memory. We fate round the Fire for the moft part of the Evening: family News and country Goffip: and *Anne* eager to relate fundry Tales of *Robin Hood*, and marvellous Stories of Witchcraft and Fairie-lore, drawing down upon herself the grave Rebuke of the *Chaplaine*, to which she gave little heed. When retired to my Closet, could not forbeare contrasting my present State with that of these light-hearted Maidens: I have not seene many more Yeares than these have, and yet such Gaiety of Spirit is mine no more, the Hand of Care presseth heavily on the young Heart, which enters upon the troubled and carefull Path of domestic Life, and upon the Duties which appertaine unto the Mistresse of a Household, before it hath had time to enure itselfe to Hardships and Disappointments, or hath had Experience of its owne Weaknesse or its owne Power: yet I would not repine; a deeper Well-spring of Joy hath beene open'd to me, though its Waters are mingled with Drops of Bitternesse. Some one sayth, our best Blessings are bought with Paine, as our highest Vertue through Sin and Sorrow: this may seeme a Mystery; but *my Thoughts are not your Thoughts, nor my Ways your Ways, saith the Lord.* Raise up and strengthen within me, O mercifull *Father* that Faith in thy perfect Wisdom and Love as shall enable me to trust in thee to direct my Ways and lead me to obey thy Will as a little child:

1640-1.

blesse and protect my *deare Husband*, and keep him in the Way of Truth and Liberty: keep in Health and Safety, O *Lord*, my precious little Ones, and uphold me in the Fulfillment of the several Duties committed to my Charge.

March 24, Wednesday.

The *Nurserie* a Scene of much Merriment this Morning. *Anne* at high Play with *Di* and *Fanny*, and *Margaret* with the *Baby*, who clapp'd her Hands and screamed with Delight. My Cousins are both good-tempered, lively Creatures, and I am vastly fond of them already, and they no lesse so of me and the Children. I tooke them over the House, and left them in the *Long Gallery*. They followed me after a while, bringing their Needlework, and I tooke my Embroidery, which has got on but slowly of late: their lively Talk made the Day passe pleasantly. After Dinner we walked down to the *Village*, calling at blind *Betty's* as we return'd.

March 25, Thursday.

Lady Day. In the *Steward's* Room two or three Houres, paying out Wages and so forth, and looking over *Armstrong's* Bookes. The last yeare's Wool was sold, the greater part thereof, to the Baize-maker at *Colchester*, at 24 Shillings the Tod, a better Price than hath been payd of late.

Lady Willoughby.

1641.

The *Great Hall* with its blazing Fire and the Women bufy at their Spinning, ever and anon finging to the hum of the Wheels, was a Sight pleafant to look upon. *Nancy* did defire fhe might have a Wheel taken to the *Parlour*, much preferring making of Thread to ufing the fame. *Margaret* is a notable Needle-woman: her Sifter brought a bright Blufh to her Cheeke by fome Query refpecting a particular Piece of Needlework in hand; and added, on perceiving the effect fhe had produced, fhe had heard S^r. *Erafmus de la Fountain* much commend the delicate Paterne: whereat poore *Margaret* attempted to look up unconcern'd, but was obliged to fmile at her Sifter's Pleafantry. I was difcreet, and led the Converfation back to the Spinning.

The Days paffe fmoothly, yet Time feemeth very long fince my deare *Lord* departed on his Journey. We heare no News. *Armftrong* will perchance gain fome Tydings at *Colchefter*: and I muft await his Return with fuch Patience I can.

Since my little *Fanny's* long Sickneffe I have continued the Habit of remaining by her at night, fometime after fhe is in Bed: thefe are Seafons peculiarly fweet and foothing; there

1641.

seemeth something holy in the Aire of the dimly lighted *Chamber*, wherein is no Sound heard but the soft breathing of the sleeping Infant. I feel at such time as if brought nearer to the *Divine Presence*, and with every Care and busy Thought gathered into Silence, almost seeme as though admitted to the Company of the Angels who keepe their appointed Watch around the little Child: one desire only filling my Soul that my Children may grow up to walk in the way of the Righteous: at such Moments too how clearly is perceiv'd and acknowledg'd the Claim of the *Creator* over the young Creature he hath formed: He hath breathed into it the Breath of Life, and made it a living Soule, and hath given it to a Mother's Keeping: she boweth herselfe before him, and receiveth from his hand this *Pearle of great price*, when the Lord *maketh up his Jewels* to be required of her againe. Sanctifie, O *Lord*, I beseech thee, these Houres of Stillnesse and Meditation to my Soule's eternal Good, and to the Fulfillment of thy holy Purpose towards us.

March 30, Tuesday.

Sitting with my two little Maidens in the *Nurserie* to-day, *Baby* asleep in the Cradle, and the Time drawing nigh for them to go to

Bed, the way opened of faying a few words to them on the fubject of Prayer, and methought it ftrengthened my owne Faith as I brought to their Remembrance that *Jefus Chrift* himfelfe pray'd, and had told us to do fo, and had taught us in what manner we fhould pray, alfo giving us Affurance that *God* would alwayes heare our Supplications, if offered in Humility and Faith: Herein fhould we find abiding Comfort and occafion of Thankfullneffe: *Diana* I thought, from the Expreffion of her Countenance, underftood what was fayd. *Fanny* look'd and fmiled and made fome childifh Remark, but poffibly tooke in fome notion of what was meant. It is a teaching Leffon, the loving Sorte of Truft with which our Children liften: how carefull fhould we be that Nothing deftroy this Confidence.

When I came downe ftaires, met *John* in the *Hall:* he brought me a Letter, and had heard divers Reports. He had the good hap to fall in with Meffengers on their road to the North, and accompanied them a mile or two on their Way to gaine what Intelligence he could. When the Earle of *Strafford* was brought from the *Tower*, he was guarded by 200 of the Train-band on his way to *Weftmin-*

1641.

ster Hall. Every day of the paſt weeke he was brought thus to and fro to the Triall. The *King* and *Queene* and the *Prince* proceeded to *Weſtminſter* about 9 of the clock: they ſat in their private Cloſet, one being encloſed on each ſide of the Throne with Boards and hung with Arras, in order that the *King* might be preſent without taking Parte, untill ſuch time as he ſhould chooſe: neverthelefſe he ſhortly brake downe with his own Hand the Trellis, and ſo ſate in the eyes of all. When the *Earle* enter'd, the Axe was not carried before him, the *King* having ſo commanded. The Reading of the Impeachment with the Lord *Strafford's* Reply occupied the firſt Day.

There was much Eating and Drinking during the Day, unſeemely Conduct in the *King's* preſence, and ill becoming the Solemnity of the Occaſion: the Sittings did oft laſt till 2 or 3 of the clock at night. Mr. *Pym* made a long Speech on the 2nd day. What ſeemeth ſtrange, in the *Galleries* were all the chief Ladies of the Court, with Pen and Ink and Papers, taking note of what paſſ'd. It is ſayd, though he was proved guilty of great Wickedneſſe and Tyrannie, yet no one Deed taken ſingly did come within the verge of

Lady Willoughby.

Treafon. The *Earle* did himfelfe fay aloud, there was nothing that could be Treafon, and if one thoufand Mifdemeanours make not a Felony, how fhould 28 make it a Treafon? So foone as the Triall is concluded, we fhall furely hear thereof.

No Letter or Meffenger yet arrived. It is well for me that nurferie Cares and Employments cannot be neglected, and I am thus compelled to exertion, though painefull Thoughts occupy my Mind. It is an awfull thing for Man to take the Life of Man, and difficult to reconcile to the Precepts of Mercy and Forgiveneffe, given by our *Saviour*, more efpecially doth it grieve me to fee the Spirit of Perfecution fo ftrong in the Minifter of Religion. The *Chaplain* and I agree not in thefe Matters, and he hath ever readie in his Mouth Texts from *Holy Scriptures* to juftify Bloodfhed: the Law of old time was an Eye for an Eye, but not fuch is the Law of *Chrift*. I do oft wifh for my *Hufband's* Prefence in his owne Family: the difcontented and fanatic Tone of Exhortation adopted of late worketh no Good: for my poore Part I fee no doing of *God's* Service in neglecting their Duty, which fome both Men and Women in the Houfehold fcruple

1641.

April 19, Monday.

1641.

not. This wresting of the old *Bible* expressions to suit different Opinions, methinks, is like to be dangerous, and maketh a Snare to the Weake.

April 24, Saturday.

The Bill hath pass'd the *Commons' House*, by a very great Majority, and is sent up to the *Lords*. Mobs of violent Men were gathered round the Parliament, crying for *Strafford's* Blood. The *Lords* made *Complaint* they were threatened: and Dr. *Burgess*, a popular Preacher, was put forth to addresse the Crowd, who thereupon dispersed themselves. The *King* is accused of endeavouring to influence the *House of Lords*, and trusts much in the Earle of *Bedford*, who it is sayd hath secretly undertooke that the Earle of *Strafford's* Life should not be forfeited.

May 7, Friday.

A Report hath arisen that the *King* hath projected the Earle's escape from the *Tower*.

So great is the Excitement that the Noise of a Board breaking in the *House* did so greatly terrifie the Members that some ran out: others thought it was another Gun-powder Plot.

May 8, Saturday.

No further News from *London*. Thoughts so distracted that to set downe some Particulars of public Events as they reach us is all that I am well able. Children at this time well in

Lady Willoughby.

Health, a great Mercy: let me not be unmindfull of this and other manifold Bleſſings; but, as the *Apoſtle* ſayth, *by Prayer and Supplication, with Thankſgiving, be my Requeſts made known unto* God.

1641.

The Bill has paſſ'd: the Majority 21 to 19: my *Huſband* ſayth many left the *Houſe*. The Earle of *Bedford*, having ſicken'd of the Smallpox laſt weeke, died on the 9th: he is a great Loſſe to all Parties, being a juſt and good Man; he hath alwayes oppoſed the perſecuting Laws againſt the Non-conformiſt Miniſters, and beene the Enemy of all arbitrary Power, and had occupied himſelfe till his Death in the endeavour to reconcile his Party to ſomething leſſe than capital Puniſhment in the *Earle's* caſe: and 'tis thought the *King* had confidently truſted in his Influence obtaining this End. The Royal Aſſent has beene given by Commiſſion. When the Earle of *Strafford* was inform'd thereof, he layd his Hand on his Breaſt, and ſayd, *Put not your Truſt in Princes:* poore Man, he hath good Reaſon to ſay ſo. The Prince of *Wales* came to the *Houſe* with a Letter from the *King*, a poore Effort to ſave the *Earle*, and to ſatisfie his Conſcience.

May 13, Thurſday.

The Execution tooke place on *Wedneſday*

May 15, Saturday.

the 12th: the crowds of People prefent were orderly, and gave way to no expreffion of Triumph; but at night it is reported they teftified their Satisfaction by lighting Bonfires, &c. My deare Life doth hope to get away in a few Days: how great will be the Joy to fee him enter his own Doore againe. He fayth the *Queene Mother* hath petition'd the *Houfe of Commons* for a Guard: fhe being fearfull of Crowds and Tumults: 'twas referred to Committee. The *Houfe* moved that the *Lords* fhould join in a Petition to His Majefty that fhe depart this Kingdome.

Have retired to my *Clofet* at an early Houre, that I may paffe fome time in the Exercife of Self-examination, efpecially fuited to the Day, the fame being that on which I was born. Firft, let me return Thanks to *Almighty God* that I was bleffed with a Pious and Tender *Mother:* 2ndly, That I have been favoured with goode Health: and thirdly, that in Wedded Life my Partner is one worthy of my deareft Affection & high Efteeme, and who hath ever treated with Gentleneffe and Condefcention my Faults and many Deficiencies. Like unto the loving them who love us is the Thankfulneffe of the Heart for thofe Mercies

Lady Willoughby.

1641.

and Orderings of *Providence* pleafant to our natural Feelings: how have I borne the Trialls and Difappointments which have beene given mee to beare? When the *Lord* tooke from me my precious Firft-born, it was as it were the Dividing afunder of Soul and Spirit, and of the Joints and Marrow: and I would not be comforted. Yet I doubt not that through this Tribulation I have in fome meafure beene brought to a more humbling Senfe of my thoughtleffe and finful State, and to the Conviction that only through Divine Grace could my difobedient and rebellious Spirit be brought into entire Submiffion and the patient taking up the *Croffe* felt to be a daily Duty. Great and oft have beene my Backflidings; yet bleffed be *God*, I hope that Faith faileth not, but doth ftrengthen and become more and more an abiding Principle of Action. Much of Indolence and Selfifhneffe I have daily to ftruggle with: yet fometimes the comforting Hope is granted, that in thefe refpects there is Improvement. Though no longer have I a deare *Mother*, yet is her Memory fo connected with my *Children* that in my own capacity as a Mother I feeme with her in many Scenes of her paft Life. Perhaps fhe doth now behold mee ftepping along

1641.

through this Vale of Teares, oft stumbling, but an unseene Arm supporting mee from utterly falling, and peacefull Resting-places and refreshing waters vouchsafed: and when I draw nigh unto the End of my Pilgrimage, where lieth the Shadow of Death, may I still feare no Evill, but know that the *Lord* is with mee. Have read the 51st and 103d *Psalmes*, and the 5th, 6th, and 7th Chapters of *St. Mathew*, and with renewed Thanksgiving after looking on the sleeping Little Ones, I will now retire to my solitary Chamber.

June 2, Wednesday.

There hath of late beene public Events of such strong Interest, that small domestic Affaires have seemed of too little Import, compared therewith, to set ought downe, and my Pen too is idly disposed. My time is mostly thus ordered: after that I have looked into ordinary household Businesse, I teach *Diana* her Reading and Spelling; she is an apt Scholar, and is becoming a notable little Sempstresse: her Temper is quick, and her Behaviour sometimes overbearing to her *Sister;* but she hath warme Affections, and soon repents of Unkindnesse or Anger: *Fanny* is more gentle and docile, but with this too readily in Teares; they are both vastly fond of *Baby*, and *Fanny* gives it oft-

Lady Willoughby.

times such a Hug with her chubby Arm as makes it cry, and then she cries too. *Fan* learns some little. In the Afternoone walke out, calling on some of my poore Neighbours, and administering to the Ailing such Remedies as I can bestow.

It is like to be a good Hay-harvest: the Women all called forth to give Helpe therein. I tooke Charge of the *Nurserie*: *Di* and *Fan* in the Field most part of the Day. Old *Bridget* died last Night; and *Smythe* now keepes to his Bed.

The Report hath reached us that the *Queene Mother* hath embarked: a good Riddance to the Countrey. It is sayd the *Queene* wished to accompany her; and under plea of Ill-health made Request to this effect to the *House of Commons*, which was refused: at the same time the *House* expressed a Willingnesse to further her Satisfaction in all things so farre as may stand with the Public Good. Methinks the *King* must be discomposed by this Opposition to the *Queenes* Wishes, which bodeth further Trouble and Vexation to him.

The *King* is still in *Scotland*, but is likely to go to *Ireland*: Rebellion and dreadfull Massacres in that unhappy Countrey.

The Bishops accused of High Treason.

1641.

June 24,
Thursday.

July 17,
Saturday.

Sept. 15,
Wednesday.

Dec. 14,
Tuesday.

From the Diary of

1641-2.

January 8, Saturday.

1641-2.

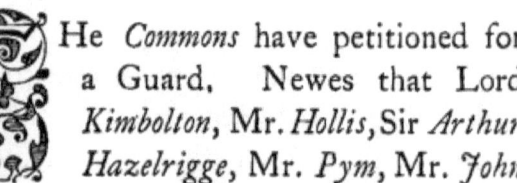He *Commons* have petitioned for a Guard. Newes that Lord *Kimbolton*, Mr. *Hollis*, Sir *Arthur Hazelrigge*, Mr. *Pym*, Mr. *John Hampden*, and another, have been accused of High Treason by the *Attorney General*. Whilst the *Lords* were deliberating, Word was brought that Officers were sealing up the Doores, Trunks, &c. of the accused Members. The *Commons* ordered their *Sergeant at Armes* to breake them open: of a sudden there came a Message from the *King* to the *Speaker* requiring him to deliver up the 5 Members. The *House* replied they would take the Matter into Consideration. The next day after Dinner, and when they had scarcely taken their Seats, Newes was brought them that the *King* was coming with Hundreds of arm'd Men and Officers; they fearing Vio-

Lady Willoughby.

lence and Strife in the House, order'd the accused Members to leave the House: which they did just in time. My *Lord* sayth the *King* knock'd hastily on the Doore, and came in with the *Prince Palatine*, leaving the arm'd Men at the Doore. The whole *House* stood up uncovered: the *King* walked straightway to the *Speaker's* Chaire, and seated himselfe therein. Then he cast searching lookes around, and not seeing those he sought, spoke in a severe Tone, asking were any of those Persons there, ending with these Words, or some similar, *I do expect, as soon as they come to the House, you will send them to me; otherwise I must take my owne Course to find them,* and arose and wentout, amidst Murmuring and cries of Privilege. This open Defiance of *King* and *Parliament* has created a vast stir: and many marvel at the bold bearing of the *House*. The next Day the *King* went into the City of *London*, when the *Common Councill* were assembled at the *Guildhall;* but made not much Impression: neverthelesse he got a good Dinner at the House of one of the *Sheriffes*.

For some days no Tidings have reached us: all that we have heard of late is of the *Militia Bill*, which is calling forth strong Feelings on both Sides. The *Queene* and *Princesse* are at

1641-2.

Feb. 28, Monday.

1641-2.

length gone into *Holland*: it is fayd fhe hath taken, befide her Plate, the Crown Jewels. The *King* returned not to *Whitehall*, but is at *Theobalds*, the Prince of *Wales* with him.

March 17, Thurfday.

This Forenoon my little Daughter *Fanny* fhowed fo wilfull and froward a Spirit, refufing to do that fhe was told, that I was forced to correct her with fome feverity: fhe hath of late fallen away from the ready Obedience wherewith fhe did formerly attend to my Bidding, and I do much reproach myfelfe in that I have beene neglectfull of my Duty towards her, and the others; thus occafioning Trouble to them, and Grief and Difappointment to myfelfe. Sorely tryed by divers Anxieties I have too much look'd to my deare Little Ones for prefent Joy and Comfort: and haply in my forlorne State, with an encreafed Tenderneffe have beene led to overlooke the Beginnings of unruly & difobedient Conduct, which ought to have met with Correction.

As I ftood and look'd on the little Face fo lately difturbed by angry Feelings now quietly afleepe, I deeply bewailed the Effects of my Selfifhneffe. *Lord*, I have beene an unfaithfull Steward, and neglected the Talents committed to me: call me not to account, Oh Righteous

Father: take not away from mee this precious Truſt: but whileſt I acknowledge and deplore my Unworthineſſe, ſtrengthen, I beſeech thee, my weake Minde, and helpe mee to traine them up in Obedience, which ſhall prepare them for a yet higher. Thou knoweſt the Burthen of theſe fearefull and troublous Times is heavy to be borne: yet would I ſtrive and pray for a more patient and faithfull Spirit.

 Attended to family Buſineſſe and Duties with renew'd Diligence: and I truſt humbled, by the paſt Experience of Slackneſſe in performing the ſame. I weary for my deare *Huſband's* preſence and Support.

 Intelligence that the *Lieutenants* of *Counties* are forthwith to organize *Militias:* the Farmers and Labouring Men will be put to great Inconvenience and Loſſe.

 Late in the Afternoone my *Lord* arrived, travaile-ſoiled, having ridden ſo farre out of his way to the North: he with ſome others are appointed to preſent to the *King*, now at *Yorke*, a Declaration from *Parliament*. He had but a few Houres to ſtay: ſo much to be ſayd in ſhort Time, we ſcarce knew where to begin: he inclined to diſmiſſe for a while all Public Affaires. I cauſed a good fire to be

March 18, Friday.

March 19, Saturday.

1641-2.

made in our favourite Parlour. *Armstrong* relieved his *Master* of parts of his Riding-dresse, and tooke Orders respecting fresh Horses, baggage, &c. the while I hasten'd up to the *Nurserie* & brought downe the three *Girls*. *Fan* tooke her old Place on her Father's Knee, *Di* on a Stool at his Feet, and I nursed and coaxed *Baby* into not being alarmed at a Stranger, so little has she seene of him, that at first she did refuse to leave my Arms for his: very great was our Satisfaction and Delight: he look'd wearied, and well he might, but sayd the sight of so many deare Faces was the onely Happinesse he had had since he last saw us, and did more to rest him than could aught else: the Dogs too shared his Notice: and the *Children* prattled so that we could hardly get in a word to each other. One by one they were sent off to Bed, and we had a short space of Quiet to ourselves. Before we are like to meete againe, he doth expect, as doe all Men, that Blood will have beene shed: both Parties are now scambling for Armes: and nothing can save this unhappy Kingdome from a Warre. Wee are much out of the way: but in disturbed Times, worthlesse and evil-disposed Persons are readie for any Violence, and under Pretext of being engaged for one Side or the other, likely to plunder the undefended: and *Armstrong* has orders to see that before dark, the House be shut, and all the Men within; who are to be armed: the new *Militia Act* will make this needfull. My *Lord* will have with him always one or more trust-worthy Serving-men, whom he can send with Letters or Messages, and heare from us in returne: and herein wee must both take such Comfort as wee can. He is now under the Orders of *Parliament*, and for some time is pretty certaine to be in the *North*, the *King* having established a sort of Court at *Yorke*. The Take-leave time came at last, *And now, deare Heart*, he sayd to his trembling *Wife*, with much adoe I kept a tolerable Composure, *have no Misgivings of thyselfe: I have ever found thee of quick Wit in Difficulties, and manifesting a quiet Courage and Endurance, at which I have marvelled: and if need should be, I will find Meanes for your better Protection.* Well was it now that the Horses were readie, and he look'd not around, after his parting Embrace, to see mee drown'd in Teares. He set forth well armed. Two Men the same, and another with a led Horse and Baggage.

Went to my lonely Roome at Night: the

1641-2.

Casement shook with the Winde, and presently the Raine came downe heavily: for a time I was overpower'd with the Grief of losing him, and thinking of him riding all night in Weather so tempestuous, the while I sat by a brightly burning Fire, in a comfortable warm Roome. Yet would I gladly share his Hardshippes, and be at his Side through all. Roused myself at last, and prepared for Rest, praying for Strength that my selfish Love may never bee a Hinderance to my beloved *Husband* in the way of his Duty, but rather that I may give all the Aide that a poore weake Creature may, to one so farre above her in all true Noblenesse. As I beheld the little Face sleeping beside mee, thought what should betide if wee were driven from our Home: how should wee find Shelter for this tender Flower, and the other deare ones.

March 22, Tuesday.

The *Chaplaine*, when wee met this Morning, with much Respect did offer his Services: he sideth with the *Parliament*, and I fancy could play the part of Soldier well, other ways than in Spirituall Warfare.

March 31, Thursday.

Had the great Comfort of a Letter dated *Nottinghame*: my *Husband* reach'd that Place soone after Sir *Anthony Ereby* and the Lord

Lady Willoughby.

Dungarvon, whom he was to meete there: and they presently departed for *Yorke*. My Husband telleth mee that Mr. *John Hutchinson* boldly opposed the Taking-away the Pouder from the *Castle* by the Sheriffe for the *Kings* Use: the which was well nigh accomplished. It did so happen that Mr. *Hutchinson* chancing to call on the *Mayor*, was there told that Lord *Newark* and the Sheriffe were up stairs seeing the Pouder weighed out. A good number of People were gathered together, and told Mr. *Hutchinson*, if he would stand by them, they would not let it be taken away: and some were minded to go up and tosse the Sheriffe out of the Windowes. Thereupon Mr. *Hutchinson* went up, and made manfull Remonstrance with the sayd Sheriffe, and they did presently put up their Papers, and left the Townes-hall. My *Lord* had some knowledge of Mr. *Hutchinson*, and is right glad to find him a stedfast Friend, on the side of Liberty and Justice.

It is no easie Matter to follow my usuall Employments, and I make some excuse continually to myselfe for looking towards the Gate, though no Newes is like to arrive yet awhile. The afternoone was fine, and I walked with the Children to *Framlingham*, and went

1641-2.

April 5, *Tuesday*.

1642.

over great part of the *Caſtle*, met there Doctor *Sampſon*, who gave me at conſiderable length the Hiſtory thereof. He was in much Concerne for his Friend Mr. *Lovekin*, the Rector of *Ufford*, who hath beene plundered of every thing ſave one Silver-ſpoone which he did hide in his Sleeve. The Oak-trees hereabout are of great ſize. The *Children* were mightily pleaſed with the *Caſtle:* and were it not that their Hunger made the thought of Supper well pleaſing to them, I ſhould not eaſily have got them away.

April 19, Tueſday.

This morning was mild & bright: the Woods clothed in the ſoft Greene of early Spring : & the whole Scene ſo quiet and beautifull, 'twas ſad to reflect how many happy country Places were defaced by the Trampling of Soldiers, & Women and Children ſitting in Terror of Warre at their very Doores. I walk'd down to blind *Betty's* Cottage: the Doore ſtood partly open: and as I entered ſhe was ſeated by the ſmall Fire, her Dreſſe cleane though homely and worne, and her poore ſightleſſe Face wearing its accuſtomed Looke of Contentment: her Lips moved, and ſhe raiſed up her withered Hand at times, as if in Supplication. She knew my ſtep, & aroſe to meet mee with her wonted Salutation of Respect and Wellcome: her first Enquiry was to know if I had heard Tydings of the Lord *Willoughby*: & then of the *Children*, every particular of their Health. And now shall I reade to you, *Betty*? I asked: with many Thankes she express'd the Pleasure it would give. The *Chaplaine* had not call'd to see her these three Daies: and a Chapter, as she sayd, would be more to her than Meate or Drinke. I read a portion of *Isaiah*, and afterward the 15th Chapter of *Corinthians*: her Remarks thereon, though simple, reminded mee in their Piety and Zeale of my deare *Mother*. She then begged for the last of *Revelations*, wherein she doth alway find peculiar Edification and Delight. This poore lone Widow is a living Sermon to mee in her Faith under all her Troubles, which have beene manifold: but they have led her to the true Source of Peace and Consolation.

Before I left my Chamber this morning, was told a Messenger had arrived from *Aldborough*, having come there by Sea from *Hull* desiring Speech of mee, saying he was from *Yorke*: I did lose no time in seeing him. He sayd the Lord *Willoughby* had not Time or Meanes to write, but sent mee his Ring as a Token that he who

1642.

bare it was to be trufted in his Relation of Affaires as they then were. On the 22nd the *King* fent the Duke of *Yorke* and the Prince *Palatine* with the Earle of *Newport* to *Hull*, without any armed Force, my *Lord* with them, as if to fee the Town: the Day following they were to dine with the *Mayor:* but a little before noone Sir *John Hotham* was informed the *King* intended to dine with him that day, and was within 3 or 4 miles of *Hull*, with 300 Horfe and more. He haftened to confult the Aldermen and fome others on the *Parliament* fide: and they fent a Meffenger befeeching his *Majefty* not to come, as the Governour could not admit him. But the *King* advanced: the Bridge was drawn up, and the Gates fhut, and the Soldiers ftood to their Arms. The *King* rode up to the Gate, and commanded Sir *John* to open the Gates: he anfwered that he was entrufted with the Securing the Towne, and would do his Duty: but if the *King* pleafed, he might enter with 12 Men: this the *King* refufed. At one of the clock the Duke of *Yorke* and others with him were allowed to go out. The *King* ftayed there till afternoone, when he gave Sir *John Hotham* an Houre to confider what he would doe, and retired: then

Lady Willoughby.

he came backe to the Gate & received the same Answer as before. Thereat he caused the Herald to proclaime Sir *John* Hotham a Traitour: and in great Anger and Disappointment the *King* went away, and lodged at *Beverley*. My *Husband* will remaine at *Hull*, being appointed with 3 other Commissioners to act with Sir *John* Hotham. The *Parliament* have voted Thanks to the Governour, and sent an Order for the Ordnance and moste of the Armes to be sent to *London*. For a short time my deare *Husband* is employed on a Service of seeming little Danger, but this cannot be for long. The Messenger stayed only for needfull Refreshment, proceeding to *London*: desired *John Armstrong* to reward him with liberal hand, and also request him to send us the *Perfect Diurnall*, or such Paper as he can procure, when he reaches *London*.

The *King*, having got Possession of the Great Seale, hath issued Proclamations commanding the People in no way to aide the *Parliament*: the *Parliament* doing the same to forbid their aiding the *King*: what can the poore People do?

There is Rumour that the *King* hath collected a considerable Force, and is gone to besiege *Hull*.

June 28, Tuesday.

From the Diary of

1642.
July 15, Friday.

The *Parliament* have issued an Order for the bringing in Money, Plate, Horses, &c. and have named the Earle of *Essex Commander* of the Army; many Gentlemen of the *House* of *Commons* have entered the Service, Lord *Grey*, *Hollis*, Sir *William Waller*, and our good friend the excellent Mr. *Hampden*.

July 16, Saturday.

The Paper says the Lord *Willoughby* is made Lord-Lieutenant of *Lincolnshire;* and Mr. *Oliver Cromwell*, the Member for *Cambridge*, is a Colonel: and will raise Forces and Money in that County and *Norfolk* and *Suffolk*.

Some part of *Suffolk* has shown itselfe in Favour of the *King*. Would that my *Lord* were at home: yet his Estates lying chiefly in *Lincolnshire*, his Presence there is doubtlesse important.

Not only have the Wealthier Sort brought in their Money, Silver Goblets, and such like, but poore Women of their small meanes, even to their Silver Bodkins and Thimbles.

Aug. 29, Monday.

The Royal Standard set up in *Nottinghame:* we heare that the *King* himselfe rode up to the Top of the Hill with the Standard Bearer: the evening was stormy, and the next morning the Standard was found blown downe: & some say it so happened a second time, and many of

Lady Willoughby.

the Royalist Party much cast downe by an Event so ominous. Poore *King*, my Heart pitieth him, as who can help? happy they who are not set in the high Places.

The *King* hath marched towards *London*: the *Parliament*, having notice thereof, ordered the Train-bands to be in readinesse, and that the *City* should be fortified with Posts and Chaines: and they say vast numbers of People, even Women and Children, came to the Worke, digging and carrying the Earth to make the new Fortifications.

Whilst that my *Lord* some while ago was raising and putting into order the *Lincolnshire* Militia, the *King* being informed thereof wrote to him desiring him to desist: whereupon he returned Answer, that it was not in his power to do that which his *Majesty* required of him, without Breach of that Trust which he had undertaken to the *Parliament*, and to which he was encouraged by the Opinion of his *Majesty's* great Officers eminent in the Knowledge of the Lawes, wherein he was not learned.

The Lord *Brooke* is actively at worke in *Warwickshire*.

Tidings of an Encounter betweene the two Armies: the first Report that our Side were

1642.

September.

Oct. 28,
Friday.

defeated: then came others that the *King's* Forces were beaten with great Loſſe. Certaine it was that a Battle had beene fought: and late in the evening I ſaw from my Bedroom Window a Man riding up, his Horſe ſtumbling from Fatigue, and preſently was told it was *Shephard*. As onely from great Neceſſitie would my *Huſband* ſend from him this truſty Man, I feared ſome ill Newes: and when *Shephard* ſaid his *Lord* was well, I could ſcarcely ſtand, ſo great was the Reliefe from that which I was afraid of hearing. A battle had beene fought at a Village called *Keynton*: Lord *Eſſex* with his Army in the Village, the *King's* halted at *Edgehill*. *Eſſex* advanced into the Plaine, and he ordered the Artillery to fire on that Part where the *King* was reported to be: and a terrible Fight began. The Royal Standard was taken: Prince *Rupert* entered *Keynton*, pillaging and committing great Cruelty: men ſayd it would have gone hard with *Eſſex* if he had not thus loſt time. My *Lord* joined them with his Regiment, *Hampden's* and another, in the height of the Conflict; they had laine on the Field all night, without Covering or Proviſions. He told *Shephard* to tell mee he could not be in better Company, Colonel

Hampden and he being much together. Some wiſhed to purſue the *King*, who is gone towards *Banbury*: others adviſed Reſt for the Soldiers. I aſked *Shephard* how my *Lord* looked, and he ſayth paſſing well, not ſo wearie, to his thinking, as when in *London*: he is to remaine one or two Dayes; and take back Linen, &c. After the firſt hurry of Feeling had ſomewhat ſubſided, I endeavoured to compoſe my Minde to a due Senſe of Thankfulneſſe that I am yet ſpared Tidings of his being wounded or even worſe: how many Wives and Mothers at this time are weeping over the Dead, or watching the Wounded & Dying: and we know not whoſe Turne will be next.

The Lord *Say's* Houſe at *Broughton* hath beene taken by Prince *Rupert*.

Dr. *Sampſon* walked over from *Framlingham*, and ſtayd Dinner: he hath heard that a ſudden Attack had beene made by the *King* on *Brentford*. Lord *Eſſex* was in the *Houſe*, which had juſt received a gracious Anſwer from the *King*, and aſking if Hoſtilities were to be ſuſpended: Whilſt he ſpoke, he heard the Sound of Cannon: he haſtily left the Houſe, and gallopped acroſſe the Park in the direction of the Sound: & he found that Prince *Rupert*, who was fol-

1642.

Nov. 2.

Nov. 18, Saturday.

1642.

lowed by the *King* and the whole Army, had taken advantage of a thick Fog, and had attacked *Brentford*, where was Col. *Hollis's* Regiment, who fought so well, the Regiments of Colonel *Hampden* and my Lord *Brooke* had Time to come up: and when the Earle of *Essex* came up with a considerable Force, he found the *Royalists* had retired, and were stationed quietly on the western side of *Brentford*. The *Parliament* is in great Indignation, and have voted they will never treat with the *King* againe.

Essex at the head of more than 20,000 Men, it is sayd, was urged by *Hampden*, *Hollis*, and others to pursue the *King*, who had retreated: but for what reason was not known, he remained still. Cart-loads of Provisions, Wine, and Ale, &c. were sent out of *London* to the Army.

Some say Sir *Thomas Fairfax* has beene defeated by the Earle of *Newcastle*.

Lady Willoughby.

1643.

March 29, Monday.

Newes from *London:* the *Parliament* have enter'd into a Negotiation with the *King*, to forme a Treaty of Peace, in order whereunto Commiſſioners have beene appointed, and are now at *Oxford*, where it is ſayd the *King* treats them with Civility. He refuſes to have the Lord *Say* and *Sele* one of the Commiſſioners, becauſe he had proclaim'd him a Traitour: and another was choſen in his place. Abroad there ſeemeth only Gloom & Apprehenſion: let mee hope that within our Home there is a brighter Proſpect: Children well, and mending of their little Faults; and when I looke backe on the Yeare juſt paſt, I ſee Cauſe for Encouragement reſpecting them. And herein is any effort at Self-diſcipline well rewarded:

1643.

the more circumspectly I endeavour to walke in the strait and narrow Way, bearing cheerfully the Crosses, and performing with diligence the Duties appointed mee, not onely is my owne Progresse in the *Christian* Path made evident in the Peace which at times I am favoured to experience: but in the encreased Care and Watchfulnesse over the Tempers and Conduct of these deare *Children*, I am Witnesse of their Growth in Virtue and Happinesse. Before this Yeare cometh to a close, haply *Peace may be in our borders, and the People shall dwell in a peaceable Habitation, and in quiet resting-places.*

Thursday. People say there was a Rising for the *King* at *Lowestoffe*, and that Colonel *Cromwell*, with 1000 Horse, came upon them unawares, and gained the Towne with small difficulty: many Prisoners taken. Hitherto this side of the Country, being mostly for the *Parliament*, has beene quiet: but now, I feare mee, we shall share in the general Disturbance.

It is confidently sayd Colonel *Cromwell* hath gone to *Norwich:* Thankfull to heare the same, I had trembled to think of him within so few miles of us.

March, Monday, There is Newes that the Lord *Brooke* hath

beene shot: I would faine hope this may not be the fact. The *King* has march'd forward to *London* with a great Army.

Armstrong heard at *Woodbridge*, when he went to the Faire on Wednesday, that Colonel *Cromwell* and my *Lord* have joined the Army at *Loughborough*, and are expected to make an Attack on *Newark*. They say *Cromwell's* Soldiers are the best ordered of any, save *Hampden's* Greencoates. The Lord *Brooke's* Death is much lamented. A party of Soldiers had taken possession of the Cathedral at *Litchfield*, and fired at the House where he then was, and the bullet struck his Head, and he died instantly. He hath left 5 Children; poore young Man, he hath soone fallen: it is a satisfaction to believe Lady *Catherine* and her Family will meet with Helpe & Protection from the Earle of *Bedford*.

All hope of present Peace is at an end. The Commissioners are recalled from *Oxford* without coming to any settlement of these unhappie differences.

Dr. *Sampson* hath seene some Letters wherein is mention of S^r. *Thomas Fairfax* having received a Shot in his Wrist, the losse of Blood was so great he lay on the ground senselesse

1643.

April 19, *Wednesday.*

May 16, *Tuesday.*

1643.

till his Surgeon came up. His Wife was taken Prisoner with the Officer behind whom she rid: and the Child after being carried on horseback for twenty houres could not hold out longer, and her Father thought would have dyed, in the frequent Swoonings she did fall into. Seeing her in so distressefull a state, he bade her Maid take her to a house he saw not farre off, where she did meet with kindly Treatment.

May 22, Monday.

No Newes of my *Husband*, but am comforted to heare that Sir *Thomas Fairfax*'s little Daughter hath recover'd and his Wife hath beene sent back by the Earle of *Newcastle* in his owne Coach, and with a guard of Soldiers. See cause to beleeve that I did most consult my deare *Husband's* ease by remaining at home, of which I have sometimes doubted.

July.

Thanks be unto *God*, I have to-day a few Lines written by my dearest *Life* in much haste. A slight hurt of his left Arme being all the injury he hath sustained in the late Fight near *Grantham*. *Burleigh* House hath beene taken by *Cromwell*. Heard with feelings of sorrow of the Decease of my honoured *Uncle*, the Lord *Noel*, at a great age. We have not met of late, but I have never ceased to love and respect him, and have at times received Tokens of his Remembrance, valuable to mee for my deare *Mother's* sake, who did entertaine for him a particular Affection.

The *Diurnall* sayth Sir *John Meldrun* was well nigh beaten at the Siege of *Newark*, the Garrison sallying forth forced him to retreate, but the Lord *Willoughby* came gallantly up with his Regiment, and beate them backe into the Towne, taking divers Prisoners and a piece of Ordnance. Deare *Husband*, how conflicting are my Feelings, one moment rejoicing in his Successe and proud of his Ability and Bravery; and then trembling for his Safety, and stricken in Conscience that I could heare of Strife and Death, with aught but Horrour and Compassion.

Further Particulars of the Siege of *Gainsborough* have reach'd us: Colonel *Cromwell* had retired to *Lincoln* to recruit his Forces, and my *Lord* was in *Gainsborough*, where he made a brave Defence, and repulsed sundry Assaults. The Earle's Force consisted of 6000 Men: upon their proceeding to set fire to the Towne, my *Lord*, to save so terrible a Distresse and Ruine, sounded a Parley, and surrender'd upon quarter after eight days: but the Enemy broke the Articles and disarm'd his Soldiers, and others that had beene sent from *Nottinghame*. He hath now gone to *Lincoln*. He is considered to have done good Service, though the Towne is lost, having made some hundred Prisoners at first Taking of the Place, some of them Men of Rank, among them the Earle of *Kingston*, who with others being sent in a close boat to *Hull*: a party of *Cavaliers* seeing them passe by, called to them to stop the Boat, which they refusing to do, they fired, and so the Earle and his Man were slaine by their owne Friends. When I shall have private Intelligence I know not, or how I beare up under this terrible uncertainty, I know not: sorely am I perplex'd when I pray unto the *God* of Peace and Love to give Successe to our Armies: can his blessing rest upon the Field of Strife and Death? Mercifull *Father*, looke with Pity on thy poore misguided Creatures, and over-rule all this Evill and Suffering to a wise and rightfull issue: and if it be possible, restore the Husband and Father to his helplesse Family: and helpe mee, oh *God*, to support whatever tryall thou mayst think fit to send mee: and in my owne Distresse may I the more seeke to aide and comfort those who are yet more afflicted than has yet beene my lot in this time of Peril.

Lady Willoughby.

In the Paper mention is made of a Conspiracy: in which Mr. *Waller* is concern'd: he is fined, and hath gain'd Permission to go abroad. Two Men have beene hang'd.

To-day my Pen must record the saddest event that next to private losse could have happen'd: *Hampden*, to whom all Men did looke up as a Patterne of Virtue and a most true Patriot, has fallen: he was severely wounded in an encounter with Prince *Rupert's* Troops, who made a sudden Attack by night. *Hampden's* active and courageous Temper could not wait the slow steps of *Essex*, and he rode up to support his Friends. It had beene confidently sayd by many that *Essex* would be removed from the Command, and *Hampden* succeed him, and his Friends strove to keepe him back from this Skirmish. He was wounded in the shoulder by two balls, and rode off the Field in the direction of his Father-in-lawes Habitation at *Pyrton*, but could not go that way, by reason of the Enemy's Cavalry, and was taken into the House of one *Browne*: here he linger'd some days in severe Torments, notwithstanding which he writ divers Letters, and died on the 24th of June, a few houres after taking the *Sacrament*, offering up fervent Prayers for his Country.

1643.

July 1,
Saturday.

1643.

We are tempted to exclaim, Why might not one so excellent *be delivered from the terrour by night, and the arrow that flieth by day?* Allmoſt it ſeemeth as a judgement from Heaven upon our Cauſe. We heare of ſome ſerious Diſaſters to our Army: *Briſtol* is deliver'd up to Prince *Rupert*, and elſewhere the *King's* Troops have beene ſucceſſefull. Sir *Harry Vane* is in the North.

July 5, Wedneſday.

Heard at *Framlingham* that *Hampden* was interred in the Pariſh Church of *Hampden*, his Regiment followed him to the Grave ſinging the 90th *Pſalme:* after ſeeing their Friend layd in the Grave, they returned ſinging the 43d, to expreſſe their Truſt in *God*, and looking to Him to deliver them and their Country from Injuſtice and Oppreſſion. Thus do they truly honour the Memory of their beloved Leader in banding together to go on with his Worke: never was there ſuch Conſternation and Sorrow at one Man's Death, as when the Tidings thereof did reach *London*, in the *Parliament*, and the People throughout the Land, as if their whole Army had beene defeated: his private Loſſe is unſpeakable.

Sept. 21, Thurſday.

As day ſucceedeth day I can only ſtrive to wait with ſome degree of Compoſure for the

Lady Willoughby.

next Reports: one of our Neighbours came up to the *Hall* to tell mee he had met with some wounded Soldiers a few Miles beyond *Wickham*, who told him Sir *Thomas Fairfax* and Mr. *Cromwell* and my *Lord* have join'd Forces, and are designed for the *North*. *Hull* is besieged by the Earle of *Newcastle:* it is sayd he had secret Correspondence with the *Hothams*, which was timely discover'd; and Sir *John Hotham* and his Sonne are sent to the *Tower*, and the Charge of the Towne given to Sir *Matthew Bointon*, the Brother-in-law of Sir *John*.

The Towne of *Nottinghame* has beene sett on fire, but not more than two or three Houses destroy'd; and the same attempted againe at divers times, fire having beene discover'd layd to barnes and other buildings; it is sayd that Women did go in companies at night, to prevent the burning, which doth seeme strange. Mistresse *Lucy Hutchinson* hath not only dressed the Wounds of many of their owne Soldiers, but also of Prisoners brought into the Castle Dungeon. I have afore-time heard her much commended as a kind Lady of great Capacity and Learning; and Colonel *Hutchinson*, who ever since he was made Governour has had to

1643.

Sept. 25, Monday.

1643.

contend with perfonal Jealoufies and Oppofition, my *Lord* faith is one of the braveft and moft honourable Men on our Side.

Sept. 26, Tuefday.

Tidings of a Battle at *Newberry*. The *Lord Faulkland* killed: he hath foone followed his once beloved Friend *Hampden* to the Grave, and doubtleffe to a world where all Differences will ceafe. He was a Gentleman of great parts and did love to entertaine at his Houfe, near *Oxford*, Men of learning and ability: he was courteous and juft to all, and did endeavour all he could to promote Peace betweene the *King* and his People. Alfo in this Battle the young Earle of *Sunderland* hath loft his Life.

Dec. 15, Friday.

For a few dayes my deare *Lord* hath ftay'd with us: and I have fome hope, now that the fevere Seafon hath fet in, that he may perchance get time to fee his Family, and fettle his Affaires: he hath now departed for *London*. He faith the Lord *Faulkland* had of late beene a changed Man: his gentle Spiritt & quick Feelings fo diftreffed, that he could not fleepe, and would oft fit long in filence, at times uttering with deep Sighs the words *Peace, Peace,* and would fay to his Friends, *the very Agony of the Warre, and the Sight of the Calamities and Defolation the Kingdome did and muſt*

Lady Willoughby.

endure, would shortly breake his Heart. He was consider'd to have sought his Death, having no call to enter into the Fight, he being *Secretary of State:* he replied to one who did urge this on him, that he was wearie of the Times, and foresaw much Misery to his Countrey, and did beleeve he should be out of it ere night: and did call for a cleane Shirt, that his Friends might find his Body cleanly arrayed. If in more of Men's Minds was this Abhorrence of Warre and Strife, how happy would it be for mankind: but others say, yes but men must first act justly, then would they meete with Mercy. This the *King* hath never done by his People, and now he must suffer: what is a Crowne, if the head that wears it is dishonoured?

My deare *Husband* well in Body, but ill at ease in Mind.

Poore Mr. *Pym* is deceased after a life of Toyle and Suffering.

From the Diary of

1643-4.

January 1, Monday.

1643-4.

He Seaſon of *Chriſtmaſſe* hath paſſ'd gloomily. At a time when Families are divided by civill Differences and many gathered round a darkened and deſolate Hearth, there is not much diſpoſition to Mirthfulneſſe. The newe Yeare hath ariſen upon a diſtreſſed Land: the Dayes and the Weekes thereof are yet in the Hand of the *Almightie:* and who ſhall live or who ſhall die we know not. Apart from the publick Diſtractions and Unhappineſſe, precious Bleſſings and abundant Mercies fill our Houſe with rejoicing and thankſgiving: not onely Life but Limbs ſpared to him who had to go forth into Battle and danger, and Nurſerie proſpering. Methought as yeſterday I ſate by a bright Fire-ſide, my three little *Daughters* playing round mee, and the deare

Lady Willoughby.

Father, though abſent, in health and preſent ſafetie, few were ſo bleſt, ſuddenly their play ceaſed, and *Di* & *Fanny* were no where to be ſeene, *Beſs* on my Knee: when hidden in the deep Bay Window, they ſung to my eare very ſweetly the Carols they had learned from the Neighbours Children: they ſtaid up to Supper, and kept up a fine Prattle.

Walked downe to *Wingfields*: the poore Mother is in a pitiable ſtate, her Son's lingering Death has worne her away, & ſhe doth long to lay her head beſide him in the Grave. Strove to comfort her, but beleeve ſhe took more in ſeeing mee ſhare her Sorrow than in any Words I could ſay. Went on to ſee the Soldier who had his arme broken, beſide other injuries; he was greatly better, and able to walke a little: he ſate cleaning his Carbine & Sword, & the Teares ran downe his Wife's pale Cheeke as he talked of againe joining the Army, ſo ſoone as he could beare the Fatigue: poore Creatures. The *King* hath ſummoned a Parliament at *Oxford*: it is reported many have left the one ſitting at *Weſtminſter*.

The *King* has beene forced to leave *Oxford*, and is gone to *Worceſter*. The Earle of *Mancheſter* and his General *Cromwell* are in the

1643-4.

January 27, Saturday.

May 31, Friday.

From the Diary of

1644.

North. This *Oliver Cromwell* riseth more & more into note.

As we sate downe to dine to-day some Horsemen were seene to approach, and Sir *Harry Vane* came into the Hall: he was on his way to *Fairlawn:* and in much kindnesse rode so farre out of his way to bring mee good Tidings of him nearest to my Heart, and of the growing Successe of the People's Friends: He is hurrying on to rejoyne the Army at *Yorke*, where are the Earle, General *Fairfax*, and Colonel *Cromwell;* a large body of *Scotch* Troopes under their old Commander *Leslie* have joined them. So soone as he was gone, retired to my Closet disturbed in Minde and Conscience: in Conscience, that I had beene ledde away by Sir *Harry's* vehement and powerfull Minde to catch something of the same Spirit whilst listening to particulars of this terrible Warfare, wherein seemeth to mee now a want of womanly Tendernesse and Pity, and sorely distracted is my poore Minde by conflicting feelings of Wife and Mother: our Duties separate us in these fearefull Times: hitherto I have remained calmly at my post, but how can I longer abide so farre from one exposed to suffering and Death, who is dearer than my owne Life? Yet have

I beene supported through times of like Anxiety in a good degree of Quietnesse & Patience: let mee pray for renewed Strength and Faith.

1644.

The *Queene* hath given birth to a Daughter at *Exeter*, on the 16th.

June 18, *Tuesday.*

The *Chaplaine* returned Thankes at morning Prayers for the Victory gained by our Army: he hath received Intelligence, it seemeth, by a sure hand, that a great Battle hath beene fought at a place called *Marston Moor*, a few miles from *Yorke*.

July 6, *Saturday.*

Some further Particulars have reached us: Prince *Rupert* has bene wholly defeated, a vaste number of Prisoners taken, as also Armes of divers sorts, Pouder-barrels, the Colours and Standards, and more than 20 Pieces of Ordnance. The losse on our part small: alas, alas, all are *Englishmen*, & Children of one common *Father*. Sir *Thomas Fairfax* his Men have received great Hurt, and himselfe well nigh lost his Life: his Brother *Charles* hath since dyed of his Wounds and lies buried there.

July 11, *Thursday.*

I have no Letter, but a Message by word of mouth, that sets my Heart at rest: Thanks be unto *God*.

The Earle of *Newcastle* hath left the Kingdome, and so it is reported hath Sir *Marma-*

1644.

Oct. 22,
Tuesday.

duke *Langdale* and others. Our Army has taken possession of *Yorke*.

It hath beene very cold of late; sharp Frost in the Nights, the Oak Leaves wither and fade and come fluttering downe with every little Blast: and the Swallows are gone away, after collecting in Flocks on the Roofe of the House, during the past Weeke.

Nov. 18,
Monday.

The Archbishop of *Canterbury* hath againe beene brought before the barre of the *House*.

Nov. 19,
Tuesday.

Great Feare and Amazement in the Countrey round at the sight of three Sunnes in the firmament, and a Rainebow with the Bend towards the Earth: & this happening on the *King's* Birth-day, many did thinke it portended Evill to him, and it was remembered that a remarkable Starre was seene to shine at noone-day, the Day whereon the Prince of *Wales* was borne: some wept and trembled, and divers both men and women did kneele downe in the roads & fields. That which did most affect my Minde was beholding the Bow, that had beene set in the Clowde as a Token of the everlasting Covenant, now appearing as it were overthrown. I had withdrawne to my Closet, when *Alice* did send to speake with mee in the Still-room: She had beene out to looke at the wondrous Sight, and was greatly perturbed: I did remaine with her till she was somewhat comforted.

Letter from *London:* Mr. *Cromwell* hath made a strong Speech in the *House*, and a Mr. *Zouch Tate* hath moved the bringing in of an Ordinance to exclude all Members of *Parliament*, whether of the House of *Lords* or *Commons*, from Command & Offices in the Army; he was seconded by Sir *Harry Vane*, and the Motion carried. A Petition from the Citizens of *London* hath beene presented, thanking the *House* for their Care over the Commonwealth. Opposition by *Whitelock* and others, who spoke against the Motion as a perilous and uncalled for novelty.

The Bill which they call the Self-denying Ordinance has past: In my Ignorance I know not what is like to be the Effect of this new Act: they say the Removal of *Essex* is chiefly aimed at.

Dissensions arise in our owne Party: fresh Discussion on the Self-denying Ordinance Bill, which has at length passed the *Commons;* but when sent up to the *Lords* was rejected. The *Commons* have named Sir *Thomas Fairfax* as General in chief in place of the Earle, and other Alterations in the Army have beene made, & partly agreed to by the *Lords*.

Dec. 11, Wednesday.

1644-5.

1644-5.

January 6, Monday.

Letter from my deare *Lord:* he writes with melancholy Heart, no Effort could save his former Friend, poore Sir *John Hotham* has beene put to death: his Son was executed the day before. Sir *John* had few Friends, he had a cold harsh manner: the *Lords* had past a Vote for his Reprieve, which being known, he did fully expect one to the last moment: but the *Commons* would not give way, the Execution proceeded.

January 14, Tuesday.

The *Chaplaine* is return'd: another of these dreadfull Executions: the *Archbishop* was beheaded on the 10th, poore old Man, he hath suffered even in this world a large measure of retribution for his past Cruelties: at the end of his Speech, when upon the Scaffold, he said he forgave all the World, all and every of his bitter Enemies; that no man could be more willing to fend him out of the World than he was to go out. Some over-zealous *Presbyterian* did preffe him with Queftions: he replied the Knowledge of *Jesus Chrift* was alone the meanes of Salvation. To the Headfman he gave fome Money, and faid, *Do thine office in Mercy.* As he knelt downe, he turned pale, thereby proving it falfe what fome were whifpering about, that he had painted his face, that he might not looke afraid. It is thought that he was brought to Death chiefly by meanes of the *Scots* Party, in their vehement and unchriftian Revenge for the Part he had taken to force upon them the *Liturgy,* and to remove him out of their way.

The *Scots* Commiffioners have obtained the fetting afide of the abhorred *Liturgy:* but *Parliament* refufes to give them any legiflative or judiciall Authority: fo the *Chaplaine* doth informe mee.

Sir *Harry Vane* is appointed one of the Parliament's Commiffioners to meete thofe of the *King* at a town called *Uxbridge.* What Mercy would it be, if a peacefull Settlement could now be entered into, of the *Countrey's* Grievances and the *King's* Claims: and this

1644-5.

would seeme not unpossible, if the *King's* Word could be depended upon. It is thought he might be brought to yeeld some Points but for the Influence of the *Queene*, which is never for good. She it was who added the Postscript to the *King's* Letter on *Strafford's* businesse, *That if he must die, it were charity to reprieve him till Saturday.*

This being my *Diana's* Birth-day, I did my endeavour to contrive for her some Amusement more than ordinary: tooke her first to my Closet, and after halfe an houre spent there in, I hope, a profitable manner, we joined the other Children. She is now eight yeares of age, mends of her little Faults, and hath gained a greater degree of command over her Temper: she is Truthfull, and showeth a tender Conscience, active and industrious, and withall can enjoy a Game of Play right well. She bids fair to be comely in Countenance and of gracefull Carriage: a Satisfaction to mee, as doubtlesse it will be to herselfe. I professe not to be indifferent on this Point for my Daughters, as some are or pretend to be: neither do I think beauty any peculiar Snare to the possessor of it, but rather contrariwise, unlesse the Minde be neglected, or is by nature vaine & selfish beyond the ordinary degree in which these Defects are shared by most: and even then such Passions are no worse than in the ill-favoured, though mayhap more conspicuous by the contrast. The three *Girls* and some young Companions made very merry.

My deare *Lord* arrived most unexpectedly: he saith there is no hope of Peace. After three weekes Negotiations, the *Parliament* have recalled their Commissioners. He looketh worne, & would faine leave all these Distractions, & doth sometimes talke of going out to *Barbadoes*: Jealousies and Bickerings increase; and he with some others, sickened with Warre and Intrigue, are readie to make allmost any Terms with the *King*. Would that our good and excellent Friend *Hampden* had beene spared: trusted by all, & wise as brave, we should have had a head to our Partie, fit to governe, & one whom all would follow. Sir *Harry Vane* in close Intimacy with *Cromwell*: he and *Fairfax* keep up the Energy and determined Spirit of the Parliamentary Partie. How small a matter it seemeth would set all right.

During the time my deare *Husband* could remaine, found not time for writing.

A long time hath elapsed since I held the

penne: the illnesse of my three Girls hath occupied mee night and day. *Fanny* began with the Measles, and had a dangerous time of it, through the Fever which ranne high, and Symptomes of Inflammation of the Lunges: and for many nights I did never undresse: *Di* followed, but thro' Mercy had the Complaint lightly: and deare *Bess*, tho' sadly troubled by the Irritation, had but little Cough. This Season of Care and bodily Fatigue, and at one time of Alarm, hath not beene without its Use and Comfort: Troubles that arise in the naturall Course of *Providence*, and are adapted to our Nature and Situation, bring with them somewhat of Peace, and oft of Thankfulnesse. We receive Paine and Sicknesse as from the Hand of *God*, and looke to him to helpe us under them: and my Minde having thus beene called off from the Contemplation of the distressefull State of this poore unhappy Countrey, is renewed in Strength. Many sweet little Sayings of the Children at different times of their Sicknesse have given mee great Encouragement respecting them: can there be ought so precious to a Mother as a sure Hope that the Spirit of her Child hath tasted of the Fountaine of living Waters? May the *Lord* helpe mee to

Lady Willoughby.

cherish these faire Blossoms of Piety & Goodnesse: and grant that they may bring forth, some thirty, some sixty fold. And, oh *God*, thou who hast made mee, unworthy as I am, to be the Instrument of thy good Providence towards these little ones, make mee daily more sensible of my owne Sinfullnesse, my owne Weakenesse, and assist mee in the Worke thou hast given mee to do. *According unto the Multitude of thy tender Mercies blot out my Transgressions: wash me thoroughly from mine Iniquity, and cleanse mee from my sinne. Create in mee a cleane Heart*, O God, *and renew a right Spirit within mee. Thou hast crowned mee with Loving-kindnesse and tender mercies: blesse the Lord, O my Soul.*

Cambden House near *Evesham*, Sir *Baptist Noel's*, has beene burnt downe to prevent the Parliament making it a Garrison. It was built not many yeares ago at a great Cost and was a noble Building.

The day so milde the Children went out, and did greatly enjoy the fresh aire, and rambling about the Fields: seated on the Bank by the Pond, they wove Caps and Baskets of Rushes. *Fanny's* dainty Hands and slim Fingers looking barely strong enough for the worke: whilst we

1645.

May.

June 21, Saturday.

1645.

were all at worke, we faw Dr. *Sampfon* coming acroffe the Field: whereupon I left them, to hear what newes he might bring. At their tender age, I like not their hearing of Fighting and Crueltie more than can be helped. I have heard little of publick Affaires fince the Battle at *Nafeby*, whereat our Army was victorious, & Colonel *Cromwell's* part much noifed abroad. Dr. *Sampfon* fays the *King's* Caufe hath fuffered more by the Letters found in his Cabinet, the fame being now made publick, than by his Defeate: many of his Friends greatly grieved thereby: his Double-dealing and Arrogance herein proved, during his Treaty with the *Parliament* at *Uxbridge*, as likewife in the *Irifh* Affaire. He has now left *Ragland Caftle*, it is fuppofed making towards the North. Prince *Rupert* delivering up the City of *Briftol* in foure Dayes, after that he had boafted he could keepe it foure Months, hath greatly incenfed the *King* againft him. Whilft at *Ragland* the *King* did give in to Hunting and other Sports, and this the while his People were fuffering, and many giving up their Property and Time in his Caufe, his very Crowne too in peril.

June 25, *Wednefday.*

Reading in the *Arcadia* the Prayer of *Pamela*: fo well pleafed therewith that I know not that I can spend my Time more profitably this morning than in copying the same, that I may have it nigh at hand.

    O all-seeing Light, and eternal Life of all things: to whom nothing is either so great that it may resist, or so small that it is contemned: looke upon my Misery with thine Eye of Mercy, and let thine infinite Power vouchsafe to limit out some portion of Deliverance unto mee, as to thee shall seeme most convenient. Let not Injury, O *Lord*, triumph over mee, and let my Faults by thy Hand be corrected, and make not mine unjust Enemy the Minister of thy Justice. But yet, my *God*, if in thy Wisdom this bee the aptest Chastisement for my inexcusable Folly, if this low Bondage bee fittest for my over-high Desires, if the Pride of my not enough humble Heart bee thus to bee broken, O *Lord*, I yield unto thy will and joyfully embrace what Sorrow thou wilt have mee suffer. Onely thus much let me crave of thee (let my craving, O *Lord*, bee accepted of thee, since even that proceeds from thee), let mee crave even by the noblest Title, which in my greatest Affliction I may give myselfe, that I am thy Creature, and

1645.

by thy Goodneſſe (which is thyſelfe) that thou wilt ſuffer ſome beame of thy Majeſtie ſo to ſhine into my Minde that it may ſtill depend confidently on thee. Let Calamitie bee the exerciſe, but not the overthrow of my Virtue: let this Power prevail, but prevail not to their deſtruction: let my Greatneſſe be their Prey: let my pain bee the Sweetneſſe of their Revenge: let them, if ſo it ſeemeth good unto thee, vex me with more and more Puniſhment. But, O *Lord*, let never their Wickedneſſe have ſuch a Hand, but that I may carry a pure Minde in a pure Body.

Having beene told that *Peggy Lydgate* was in trouble, I ſett forth early as it was farre to walke. Tooke with mee the young Greyhound. Reſted awhile at the Bridge, ſaw many Fiſh, and a Water hen with her young ones paddling about at the Water's edge by the tall Reeds. The King-fiſhers did uſe to frequent hereabout, but they came not in ſight to-day: feare mee they have beene killed or frighted away: the People deem it lucky to poſſeſſe them, and hang them up in their houſes. Further downe where the ſtreame narrows ſtayed againe to hearken to the pleaſant

Lady Willoughby.

Sound made by the Water running with little splashes amid the stones, and keeping up a chearfull rippling noise as it went on its way through the Meadow below. The Doore of the Cottage was open, *Peggy* was seated on a low stool, her Face covered with her Apron, the 2 Lads standing by her. The poore Creature hath cause enow for trouble, both her Sons would be Souldiers, the elder in the *King's* Army, whilst the younger would join the Parliament Forces, some of his Kinsfolk having a yeare agone followed Mr. *Oliver Cromwell;* so in all likelihood would the Brothers meet in fight against each other. They did appeare moved by their Mother's griefe, the youngest methought shewed some tokens of yielding. I bade him follow mee good part of the way home and have hope that a few words I then spake would prove of some availment.

Armstrong mett *Robert Lydgate,* he sayd his Mother tooke on so, hee had not the heart to leave her: his Brother was gone.

My *Lord* telleth mee he met with Colonel *Hammond,* who was at the taking of *Basinghouse,* and made Prisoner there: he and another Officer were taken before the House was

1645.

Aug. 16,
Saturday.

Oct. 20,
Monday.

1645.

attacked, by a Party stealing out therefrom on a foggy night. Lieutenant General *Cromwell* wrote a Letter acquainting the Governour that if any violence were offered these Men, the best in the House should not expect Quarter. The Countesse of *Winchester's* Gentlewoman and Waiting-woman were killed by a cannon shot. Sir *Marmaduke Rawdon* declared to the Marquesse who proposed to surrender, he would not, so long as a dog, or a cat or rat did remaine: yet it would seeme there was not much Danger of such Extremity, there being found in the Castle vast store of Wheat, and 300 Flitches of Bacon, and forty thousand pounds weight of Cheese, besides Beef. They took off the Lead from the Turrets, to use for Bullets: and the Marchionesse with her Ladies did helpe to cast them. There were within the Castle 600 common Soldiers, most whereof Papists, and fought desperately. *Inigo Jones*, the great Builder, is one of the Prisoners. So likewise was *Winceslaus Hollar* who did make his escape. He is one well skilled in the Arte of engraving on Copper. My Lord *Arundell* did once show mee some small Figures by him, of Women of divers Condition and mode of Apparell, accurately designed from the Life,

Lady Willoughby.

1645.

Merchants' Wives, Country-Women, and the like. *Hollar* had Loſſe of his Patron when the *Earle*, who brought him to *England*, accompanied the *Queene Mother* and did remaine in Foreign Parts: the *King*, having look'd coldly on him ſince the Affaire of *Strafford* he did not incline to returne. Alſo it is ſayd his *Majeſtie* was offended by his boldneſſe of Speech on ſome occaſion, maintaining his own Right, albeit oppoſed to the *King's* Wiſhes. Colonel *Hammond* ſayth, the Marqueſſe, on ſome Quarrel with Sir *Marmaduke*, he being of the *Engliſh* Church, and the Marqueſſe a Roman Catholick, became ſuſpicious of him being the Governour, and had him removed: and ſhortly thereafter the Houſe was taken, the Storme not laſting more than an houre. The Silver plate, Cabinets, Jewells, and other Treaſure did afford rich Plunder: the Houſe is burned down to the Ground.

Greatly ſurpriſed to read in the *Perfect Diurnall*, that the *Houſe* has moved that the Lord *Willoughby* be made an Earle, and the ſame of other Lords, and that the Earles of *Eſſex*, *Pembroke*, &c. be made Dukes: in all likelihood the matter will end here. They whoſe Titles are of long Deſcent, methinks, would not confider newe ranke, given under the circumftances, as any addition to their Dignitie. We heare an *Englifh* Barony is to bee conferr'd on Lieutenant General *Cromwell*, with an Eftate of 2500 Pound yearly.

A Neighbour of the blind Widow came up at Noone to fay the poore infirme Creature did appeare neare her laft Houre: went ftraightway to her Cottage, fhe was ftill fenfible, and did expreffe great Satisfaction at my coming: fate fome time by her Bed-fide, fhe fpoke of her Sonne, whom fhe yet beleeves living, and ftrong were her Supplications that Divine mercy might be extended to him, that he might turne from the Evill of his Wayes, even at the Eleventh Houre: My poore prodigal Sonne, thus fhe fpake, hath he in that diftant Land, away from his poore old Mother, call'd to Minde her Words, her Prayers, and return'd to his Heavenly Father, faying, *I have finned in thy fight, and am no more worthy to be called thy Sonne.* If the Lord in his Mercy would give mee this hope, then would his unworthy Servant depart in peace. She feemed comforted: and repeated at intervals, *With God all things are poffible.* I left her in her awful Paffage from Life unto Death, a paffage to her

Lady Willoughby.

deprived of Terrour, for her Faith forsooke her not, but rather burned brighter and brighter, even to the End: she did not live through the night. Her Gaine is my Losse: though poore and meane, I have failed not to find in her Company Edification and ofttimes Comfort.

The *King* hath fled by night from *Newark* to *Oxford*: the two *Houses* have againe resolved to submit to him certaine Propositions.

My *Lord* hath heard that the young Earle of *Carlisle* hath establish'd his Claime to the *Barbadoes* Property, and is inclin'd to enter into Negotiation concerning the same. Present Perill in fighting or strife, or Perill of the deepe waters and pestilence, whichsoever way I turne Trouble on every side.

An Order hath pass'd that the Summe of 3300 pounds be paid to the Lord *Willoughby*, which I am sure the sayd Lord much needeth.

The Children greatly pleased with a tame Squirrel sent them by the old Man at the Mill. Three Turkies and a Basket of Fish came up this day from *Martins'*.

Latham House in *Lancashire* is taken: the Lady *Derby* having defended it two yeares: the Earle in the *Isle of Man* by the *King's* command. For 9 Months together the be-

1645.

Oct. 23,
Thursday.

Dec. 9,
Tuesday.

1645.

sieged Party held Communication with their Friends by meanes of a Dog, in this way: they tied a Letter round his Throat, and he went to where he did use to live, 3 miles off: here he was kept, and when any Papers were to be sent, his Mistresse tyed them in like manner, and having kept him awhile a hunger'd, open'd the door and beat him out, when he set off and returned to his Master, who was in *Latham House*. He was at last shot by a Souldier, but got to the Mote-side near the Gate, and there died. The House is burnt: the rich silk Hangings of the Beds were torn to pieces, and made into Sashes. This history of the Dog was related to mee by one there present.

Dec. 18, Thursday.

Great Disagreement in the *House*: the *Scotts* take the Side of the Presbyterians. There seemeth no Master-minde to give a steady Direction to the Power they have gained. General *Cromwell* & *Fairfax* are away from *London*, deeming it most prudent, as they hold out, to bring the rest of the Kingdome into subjection to the *Parliament*, before they besiege the *King* at *Oxford*. People remark that other Generals shut themselves up in Winter-quarters, but this *Cromwell* sets at Defiance the Cold of Winter, Stormes and Darknesse.

1646.

Aſt weeke *Fairfax* & *Cromwell* reached *Newberry*, a place within a ſhort diſtance from *Oxford*, and where the Lord *Faulkland* was killed, whereupon the *King* fled from that City in diſguiſe: ſurely brought to this extremity he would yeeld to his *Parliament*, and keepe to his Engagements. He hath made a Treaty with the *Scots*, through his Agent *Montreuil*. I do heartily wiſh they may convey him in ſafety to *Scotland*, and thence beyond Seas, there to abide for a time, till the heate of Men's Spirits againſt him paſſe away, and haply then Affaires might be ſettled for his returne to his Kingdome. The Prince of *Wales* is ſayd to have eſcaped. My deare *Huſband* is wearie of the Confuſion, and apprehendeth an

From the Diary of

1646.

Army may in the ende be more tyrannical and a worfe Enemie to contend with than a King.

June.

It is fayd the poore defeated *King flits like a hunted Partridge* from one Garrifon to another; the laft Report was of his being at *Newark*. The Princes *Rupert* and *Maurice* have demanded Paffeports of *Parliament* to go beyond feas. The *Commons* readily complyed, with Thankfulneffe to get rid of one who hath fhed fo much *Englifh* Blood. Prince *Rupert* hath latterly fhewne great Difrefpect & contemptuous Manner to the *King*.

July 20.

On the 15th Parliament fent Deputies to the *King* at *Newcaftle*, with an Addrefs containing Propofitions expreffing their wifh for Peace.

Auguft 19, *Wednefday*.

Sitting yefterday toward evening at the Bay-window, in great Abftraction of Minde, oppreffed by a fenfe of my lonely Condition, I did weepe unreftrainedly, knowing not that I was perceived by any, until a little Hand was put into mine, and *Lizzy's* face was rayfed up to kiffe mee. Sorrowfull Thoughts could not be at once fet afide, and I did not fpeake to her for a time, for my Heart was heavy. She fate quietly downe at my Feet with a gentle loving looke and fo remained. The Raine had ceafed and the Sunne fhon in through the fide cafement. The Light as it fell upon her golden Haire made her feeme like to the holy Children in the *Italian* Pictures. Of fuch, methought, are the Kingdom of Heaven: thus looketh, and haply is even now nigh unto mee, feparated only by this veil of Flefh, the Spirit of my precious Child: as the Flower of the Field fo he perifhed, & my Heart yet yearneth after him, my Firft-borne. Arofe and tooke *Lizzy* in my armes and held Her up to the Window. A few pale flowers of the Mufk Rofe fmelled fweetly after the Raine. *Di* and *Fanny* were running on the Terrace: wee went out to them, and they were as merrie as Birds: and I did put from me my own Griefe. Very gracious is the *Lord* unto me, and in him will I truft.

Had occafion to looke for fome Papers wanted by the Steward, having relation to the Eftates in Lincolnfhire, which I thought to find in the Cabinet, prefented to mee by my honoured *Father* on my Marriage. Found them not therein, opened a little Drawer which did containe a Box made of the Wood called Sandal of a fweet Perfume, a fmall piece of Amber, and a Signet Ring of wrought Gold curioufly graven, which if I mifremember not Sir *Henry*

August 22, Saturday.

1646.

Wotton did bring from *Italy*. In another Drawer was a sprig of Rosemarie, how much hath come to passe since the day whereon I tooke it with mee in sadnesse from the desolate room where my deare *Mother* departed this life! she went to a timely Rest.

August.

Newes hath arrived that *Fairfax* has taken *Ragland Castle* in *Wales*. The old Marquesse held out bravely more than ten dayes, but at length surrender'd: as many as eight hundred People and Souldiers march'd forth the Castle, which I have heard say is a noble Building. The Marquesse was accompanied by his Sonne Lord *Charles*, the Countesse of *Glamorgan*, & Lady *Jones*. How great a change for this venerable Nobleman, who but a short time since did entertaine with princely Magnificence and Loyaltie his Sovereign: and now both *King* and Subject are Wanderers. Beside losing his Castle, he is like enough to lose large summes of Money which he hath lent the *King:* high & low, Misery is all over the Land.

Sept. 16.

The Earle of *Essex* died on the 14th.

Lady Willoughby.

1646-7.

THe *Scots* having received the Summe of 200,000 pound, have march'd out of *Newcastle*, leaving the *King* to the Commissioners of *Parliament*, the Earles of *Pembroke* & *Denbigh*, and the Lord *Montague*, and the Commissioners of the House of Commons. It tooke 36 Carts to carry the bags of Money to *Yorke*, and some say it did take nine or ten dayes to count the same.

The poore *King*, a Prisoner in his owne Kingdome, is now established at *Holmby House*, and hath expressed his Satisfaction with his Treatment there and Accommodation, with one Exception, that he hath no Chaplaine, the which he petitioneth for, but it is not thought safe or expedient, & they who have taken the ordering of this Businesse have sent him Chaplaines of

January 28, Wednesday.

Feb. 19, Friday.

1646-7.

their owne Perfuafion, but the *King* will not liften to them, neither will he permitt them to fay Grace at his Table: Men fay he beareth his Misfortunes, which truly are many, with Dignity and Cheerfullneffe.

March 10, Friday.

My deare *Hufband* hath much Turmoile in the Houfe. The Earle of *Warwick* doth aime to get the three Earles, *Bedford*, *Hollande*, and *Clare* admitted: the which others would if poffible prevent, and they talke of getting the *Commons* to bring in an impeachment of the Lord of *Hollande*, on fome Affaire which my *Hufband* calleth the Forreft-bufineffe, of which I know not: befide this he went over to the other Party, notwithftanding that he had taken the Oath.

May 12, Wednefday.

The Lord *Lifle* hath beene removed from the Government of *Ireland*: and likewife his Brother *Algernon Sydney* from *Dublin*, the latter on the Motion of old Sir *Henry Vane*. This fudden removal of his Sonnes will no doubt be difpleafing to the Earle of *Leicefter*, though he keepeth himfelfe in much privacy at *Penfhurft*, and meddleth not in publick Bufineffe.

May 14, Friday.

Yefter night did receive a Letter from my Sifter *Albinia*, wherein fhe doth expreffe much tender Solicitude and Affection. Let mee be duly thankfull for the Love of so many deare Friends. Children through mercie keepe well. Have observed with satisfaction that *Fanny* hath of late shewn more Denial of Selfe. This day I did note an instance, though in a small matter. *Alice* had made two shapely Pincushions of watchet coloured Brocade, & as is too much her wont did give *Fanny* the one of most curious Device & Workmanship, who quickly perceiving some Disappointment to be felt by her Sister, with winning manner did prevaile upon her to exchange Gifts. I did refraine from bestowing Commendation, believing it to be our Duty to leave undisturbed by humane Praise, the appointed connexion of inward Peace with the performance of Duty. By the contrarie practice we encourage the growth of that, which hereafter we strive to up-root, the seeking the Praise of Men rather than the Praise of God.

On Saturday the 5th the *Commons* sate long, and because of the greatnesse of their Businesses they resolved to sit even the next day (Sunday). They did desire the *Peers* to do so likewise, which they, expecting some great Matter, agreed to do. Mr. *Algernon Sydney* did tell my *Husband* that when the *Commons* met, Mr.

June 10, *Thursday.*

1647.

Marshall their famous Minister did pray for and with them, and that when he ended his Prayer, the *Commons* desyred him to make a repetition of his Sermon which he had preach'd that day at *Westminster*. The same being over, the *Commons* rose without doing any thing, and without sending so much as a word to the *Lords*.

June 24, Thursday.

Much Discontent rising up: the *Presbyterian* Party have proclaim'd the establishment of their Form of Worship to the exclusion of every other. My *Lord* becometh more & more dissatisfied with the Spirit of Bigotry which has of late gathered such Strength, and the Self-exaltation, as exclusive as that of Popery, which they do condemn in others. This is most contrary to my deare *Husband's* naturall disposition and former Principles. It is proposed to reduce the Army, and some Troops have been disbanded.

June 25, Friday.

The Army is greatly incensed, and hath broke up its Quarters at *Nottinghame*, and march'd, People say, upon *London*. Alas, must more blood be shed? What will become of this unhappy Countrey: no King, no Rulers, and a large victorious Army set in opposition to the now feeble power of a misguided and fanatic House of *Commons.* And woe is me, the Husband whom I love and honour, so mixed up with them that he must abide by their acts, and share in them.

The Earle of *Northumberland* hath had permission to take the *King's* Children to see their Father: coming to *Caversham,* we are told a great number of People flocked thither to see them, & strewed the way with greene branches and herbes. Poore Children, their pitifull Condition moveth many hearts, & no marvell; many will in secret rejoice that this drop of comfort is permitted to the unhappy *King.*

The monthly Fast: met with the Remark following, which seemeth much to the purpose: *Let thy religious Fast be a voluntary Abstinence, not so much from Flesh as Fleshly Thoughts. He fasts truly that abstains sadly, grieves really, gives cheerefully, and forgives charitably.*

Alice becometh daily more infirme, and is but little able to take any oversight: think to place my own Waiting-woman more in charge, after she hath given some Instructions to *Patience,* who is apt at her needle, and will suit me well-enough.

As I came up from the Dairie met the Children full of Sorrow that a poore Partridge

June 28, Monday.

1647.

had beene killed by a Scythe, whilſt ſitting on her Neſt: the Egges are put under a Hen, and the Men think will be hatch'd in a few dayes.

Aug. 3, Tueſday.

Voted in the *Houſe* that the Army ſhould not come within 40 Miles of *London*.

The Army, they ſay, hath made *St. Alban's* their Head-quarters, & have ſent up to accuſe *Hollis, Stapleton, Maynard*, and others.

Great Tumults in *London*. The Speakers of both *Houſes* and great part of the Members have put themſelves under the Protection of the Army. Sorely perplex'd, & know not what is the meaning of theſe diſturbances, or what may befall my *Huſband:* the Children, too young for care, are as happy as May-queenes.

Aug. 12, Thurſday.

One Day cometh, and then another, and yet no Tidings: this is hard to endure, ignorant what may betide us in theſe evill Times.

Aug. 14, Saturday.

Late to-night my deareſt Life rode haſtily up: he was ſafe for the preſent moment, & my firſt Feeling was of unmix'd Thankfullneſſe to Him who permitted us to meete once more. After he had reſted awhile, he entered into ſome Relation of the late Events in the *Houſe*. He and many others have believed that the Power of the Army endangered the libertie of the Countrey, and the Common Council of *London*, united with them, and met, and sent a Letter to the Generall declaring their wish for Peace, and entreating that the Army might not advance, nor intermeddle with the Rights and Privileges of the *City*. The Train-bands were ordered out. Some Members met in either *House*, but the Speakers came not: and to my *Lord's* Amazement he was chosen Speaker, *pro tempore*, and Mr. *Pelham* of the *Commons*. They proceeded to appoint a Committee of Safety: and the *City* issued a Proclamation to the effect that they desired a happy and speedy Peace, by the Settlement of true Religion, & the re-establishing his *Majesty* in his just Rights and Authority. But the Proceedings of the *House* were marked by uncertainty and trepidation, & the day following, *Fairfax* came up to *Westminster* attended by *Cromwell* and regiments of Horse and Foot. The Generall on horse-back with his Life-guard, then the Speakers and Members of the *Lords* and *Commons* in coaches, and another regiment of Horse brought up the rear. Mr. *Whitelock* writes, the Officers and Gentlemen, and every Soldier had a branch of lawrel in his hat. The Generall received the Thankes of both *Houses*, and was made Lieutenant of the Tower: & thus the Army asserted its Supremacy.

For a time the consideration of our private Affaires was set aside, in the momentous concerns of this distracted Kingdome. Who will arise with a strong minde & pure Heart, to bring these struggles for Freedome, and these conflicting Opinions to a happy issue? There is one my *Husband* sayes who lackes not the will to become Leader, or peradventure the power: but none have penetrated his heart, or know if he may be trusted. I did once behold this *Cromwell*, who maketh so many quail before him, but methought his Looke was hard and cunning, and I liked him not. And the *King*, deare *Husband*, I asked, is he safe, will he depart the Countrey? No Man knoweth, he reply'd: he will not be permitted to leave the Countrey, if Guards and strong Castles can prevent. He is safe, so far as concerns his Life: he may be deprived of Power or even of his Crowne, but on no Plea can they take his Life: and yet who shall say where they will stop? I would lay downe my Life to know him to be safe; we have fought and striven, and have set a Stone rolling that haply will crush all that come

Lady Willoughby.

in its way, Laws, *Parliament*, or even the *King* himselfe. My *Husband* leant downe his Head on the table, and hid his Face on his arme, and so remained overwhelmed by the prospect of Misery before us. I ventured not to speake: it is an awfull thing to behold the Spirit of a strong Man shaken, and to hear Sobbes burst forth from his over burthened Heart. At length such violent Shivering seized him that I summoned *Armstrong*. We endeavoured to persuade him to drinke a little Wine, he tooke some, but begged for Water, his mouth was so parch'd: after some time he went to bed, and desired that *Armstrong* might sit up by him during the first part of the night, his owne Man, having had poore rest of late: he feared to affright mee by his uneasie sleepe. I layd mee downe in the Nurserie, rising oft to see if he slept: toward 3 of the clock he was more quiet: and at 4 I sent *Armstrong* to bed, and tooke his place by my poore *Husband*. I look'd on his altered Countenance, sunk & pale, the faire Brow wrinkled, and his long black Haire now gray and disorder'd: a slight quivering of his Lippes and unequall Breathing betoken'd still uneasy rest: my Eyes grew blinded with Teares, and I bent downe and

1647.

hid my face on the Pillow beside his. And here to my surprise found I had dropt asleepe: he seeming likely to remaine quiet, I arose softly and stepp'd into my Closet, and there, alone, endeavoured to compose my Thoughts: had he not been preserv'd in many Battles and dangers, and should I now give up Faith in the good Providence of *God*, beleeving heartily that we are safer in his Hands than if we could take the ordering of our Fate into our owne? I would faine have my deare Life depart hence with speed, but untill he knoweth what Course the *Parliament* will hold towards him, and those with whom he hath acted, he is unwilling to leave the Kingdome: he hath Enemys in the House of *Commons*, but likewise good Friends, & he doubteth not receiving timely Notice of any measure to his Hurt. It would ill beseem his Wife to counsel flight, nor would I, how great soever my Feares, if he could doe ought for his *King* or Countrey by remaining: but this Subjugation of the *Parliament* by the Armie, will bring the Countrey under the fierce and uncertaine Rule of the Souldiers and their Commanders, and there is no party to withstand them. I strive to put from mee the dreadfull Vision of the Scaffold and the

Lady Willoughby.

Block, which hath often vifited mee in the night-watches when fuch danger exifted not, but now may well fill my Soule with Terrour. I will befeech him to paffe over to *Holland*, he fayeth the worft will be Imprifonment in the Tower: but how many are led therefrom onely to their Death.

Word brought by a fure hand that it is order'd by the Houfe of *Peeres*, that the Lords impeach'd by the *Commons* be brought up to anfwer to the Impeachment. Friends of my *Hufband* advife him to keepe out of the way untill the prefent Heate & ftorme be a little paft over: this Counfell but ill receiv'd by him, and he is bent upon appearing.

The *King* hath efcaped from *Hampton Court*: the Report is, that he having retired to be private, as hath been his cuftome a fhort fpace before evening Prayers, and ftaying fomewhat longer than ufuall, it was taken notice of, and not yet coming forth, fuddenly there were Feares of the caufe hereof, which were encreaf'd by the crying of a Dog within, he had latterly kept conftantly with him a favourite Greyhound, often faying he did prefer them to Spaniels, upon Search being made, it was found the *King* had departed by a back Doore

1647.

Sept. 11,
Saturday.

Nov. 13,
Saturday.

1647.

which ledde to the Garden. I do heartily hope he may get away: methinks he will then ftand in a more honourable pofition to make Termes with his *Parliament* than when fhut up as a Prifoner: and the People finding themfelves without a King, perchance may wifh for him back. It is currently believ'd that fome Officers of the Armie did fecretly communicate with the *King*, and had Inftructions from Generall *Cromwell* himfelfe and others, that if he would affent to their Propofals, which were lower than thofe of the *Parliament*, the Armie would fettle him againe on the Throne: and it is thought he was hereupon inclined in his owne Judgement to enter into a Treaty with them, but was difwaded by the Bifhops. Some are as hotly againft *Cromwell* as againft the *King*: nay fome goe fo farre as to fay he was in danger of being fent to the Tower, had he not left *London* before they were prepared.

Made the needfull preparations for my Departure: my ftay in *London* muft of neceffitie bee uncertaine: wearied by much Toyle and Care, but Duty clear, is a Help through difficulties. The Morrow is a day of Reft, and will bee a feafon of Comfort and renewed Strength if ufed aright.

Lady Willoughby.

1647.
Nov. 24,
Wednesday.

This being a day whereon the *Parliament* sate not, the Lord *Gray* and *Henry Willoughby*, a young Kinsman of my Husband's, tooke mee to see some Tapestrie Hangings in the House of *Peeres*. A Portrait of Sir *Ambrose Willoughby* is work'd therein, who was Uncle to the late Lord, & Grandfather to *Henry*. They did persuade mee to be carried in a Sedan-chaire: I was well pleased to get out againe, being much discomfitted by the jolting. After some examination we discovered the Portraite, on the border under the Armes of the Lord High Admiral: it is of oval shape, a Gorget of plate armour over his Doublet, and a picked Beard and Mustachoe, like to those now worne. He was in Command of a Ship against the *Armada*. I was faine to aske whereabout my deare *Husband* had heretofore sate, but when the Thought arose, that the next time he would enter that House it would be as a prisoner to be tried by Men, many of whom were his bitter Enemies, I could scarce raise my Voice: the Lord *Gray* suspecting wherefore I look'd around so wistfully, did kindly point out the Place.

Nov. 30,
Tuesday.

To-day my *Husband* occupied himselfe for my satisfaction in drawing up a Letter to the

1647.

House of *Lords*, something to this effect: begging their Lordships would be pleased to order his Enlargement, seeing that he had beene committed without any particular Charge against him: that he had received counsell of his Friends that he is not fit for publick Employment, and was therefore resolv'd on Privacy: that he had allwayes beene faithfull to the *Parliament*: and desired their Lordships to make an honourable Construction of his Wish for Retirement. After all our Toyle, I much feare he will not at present send his Remonstrance; whensoever sett free he would without delay imbarke for *Holland*. He can no longer act with the *Parliament*, since they will make no Termes whatsoever with the *King*, and he is jealous that the Monarchy is in danger of being wholly lost, and all Rank destroyed.

Dec. 2, Thursday.

Wente downe in a coach to the Parliament-house, and sate therein the while *Henry Willoughby* did try to learne some Newes. After waiting more than an houre, the Lord *Say* came out and inform'd mee a Message had beene sent to them by the *Commons* that morning praying for further Time to be allowed for bringing up the Impeachment of the seven Lords, which was granted. Hereupon I went backe to the

Tower to tell my *Husband* of this further Delay: and it was agreed betweene us that it were well I should returne to *Parham* forthwith: and as Mistresse *Gage* did purpose to sett forth early in the forenoone to morrow, and would goe by *Hengrave*, & had offered to carry mee with her in her coach, it seemed too favourable an opportunitie to be miss'd, although it would make my Departure sudden. Left the *Tower* before 8, the Snow lying thick upon the Street, and with sorrowfull Heart made Preparation for setting forth homewards. My deare *Husband* maketh light of his situation, and strives to cheere mee, and persuade mee to take Hope in the Exertions now making by a few faithfull Friends of Influence in the *House*, who promise they will doe him what Service they can to pacifie his Adversaries, who are the more sharply bent against him. The chearfull and composed Demeanour he did maintaine served for a time to lighten my Forebodings, and the moment of Parting came on a sudden, and I followed the Guard downe the Staires and under the Archway as in a Dreame: the Doore closed after mee: had I in truth left him, my dearest Life, in that dark Prison-house there alone to await his Sentence? I knowe not how I

1647.

reach'd my Lodging, some kind Friend put mee into a coach & supported mee to my chamber.

Nature would have her way for a time, but the *Lord* suffered mee not to be wholly cast downe, and in spreading my Sorrows before Him, and committing my beloved *Husband* to His Keeping, who hath the power to save even to the uttermost, I was strengthened, and did endeavour to submit with patience to the present Triall, though it is indeed heavy and grievous to be borne. The night was cold, and my condition forlorne and comfortlesse, but I laid me downe on the bed in as much quietnesse of spirit as I well could, feeling that rest was needed to encounter the morrow's Journey from this weary Citie to returne to my poore Children. Reflection on the Encouragement given by divers kind and powerfull Friends was very helpfull, and I slept. The time of our Departure the next day was appoynted at an early houre.

Lady Willoughby.

1647-8.

NO Tydings from *London*. Newes of great Diforder and Tumult in *Canterbury*. The Mayor endeavouring the execution of the Ordinance for abolifhing Holy-days, he was much abufed by the People on *Chriftmaffe-day*, they beat him on the head, and dragg'd him up and downe. The like Violence hath beene practifed at other Places, but none hereabout. Some fewe People came into the Parke, and collected around the old Thorn, which hath many times put forth a fewe Bloffoms on *Chriftmaffe-eve*, & which they looke upon as a Miracle, but no perfon did moleft them.

The Children were abroad fo foone as the Sunne rofe, and brought in Ivy and branches of Holly, which they put about the *Hall* &

From the Diary of

1647-8.

their *Nurserie*, as their pleasure is. They set up a great Shout when there was seene a fine piece of Misseltoe at the top of a Hamper containing Apples, timely sent by their Uncle from *Gloucestershire*. I could not beare to sadden their Pleasure by the trouble of my owne Heart, and they did spend a right merrie *Christmasse*. Their Uncle *William* and his Family staying with us.

Jan. 11, Tuesday.

It is well for mee the Children give mee full Occupation: they take well to their learning, and the *Chaplaine* saith *Fanny* maketh goode progresse in the Latine; but I find her somewhat averse to Needleworke, wherein her Sister *Diana* is more expert, as also in some other Matters which in my judgement are like to be of more Service than a knowledge of Latine: though where Nature hath given a Capacitie for such studies, methinks we should err in not providing Meanes of improving the same: and I doe already see in *Fanny* an encrease of Steadinesse at her taskes, and exactnesse in the Performance of them.

Jan. 29, Saturday.

Hear from Sir *Harry Vane* the charge against my *Husband* pass'd the *House* on the 27th, and was ordered to be sent up to the Lords.

Feb. 20, Monday.

Armstrong returned yesternight from *Ald-*

Lady Willoughby.

borough: no Veſſell, it is ſayd, will ſail to *Holland* from that Place or *Yarmouth* for ſome time.

My deare Life, Thanks be unto *God*, is ſafe, his Letter is writ from the *Hague:* he hath ſeene the Prince of *Wales*.

Deare Heart,

After a toylſome Paſſage we landed at *Dort:* methought the Voyage did too nearly picture my troubled and uncertaine Life. I am well in Health: the Packet came ſafe to hand, and I was right glad of the Paſtie and Wheaten-loaf, after having ſpent the night on deck, the Victuals on board being ill to eat. The Doublet worked by my ſweete Wife did greatly add to my Comfort, as did divers other Matters lovingly remembered by her for my uſe. Heretofore, though often ſeparated, yet was I in the ſame Countrie that did contain my little Ones and her who is my Soule's Joy and Conſolation, the trueſt Friend and Counſellor that ever Man had: now each wave carry'd me onward to a ſtrange Land, & never did Abſence appear ſo unſupportable. Kiſſe our deare Children for me. Bid *Armſtrong* be carefull to omit

1647-8.

March 6, Monday.

A portion of the letter apparently alluded to by Lady Willoughby.
 Editor.

nought that I left in his Charge; he would doe well to see *Wingfield* concerning the gray Horse, which should be cared for: my Brother can ride *Berwick*.

Lady Willoughby.

1648.

Ave receaved no further Newes of my *Lord* since I heard from him that he was made *Vice Admirall* in the Duke of *Yorke's* Fleete. There is a report that the *Duke* has saild for *Holland*.

A Friend doth write that a Letter from the Prince of *Wales* to the Speaker of the *Lords* has beene read in the House, giving assurance that he will endevour his part with the *King* for a good Settlement: Also he speakes of divers marchant Vessels seized; one of these Ships it was understood was full of Gold, and was captured by the Lord *Willoughby*. I have this satisfaction in that as he doth hold this publicke Station, should any great mis-

Aug. 15, *Tuesday.*

Aug. 16, *Wednesday.*

1648.

chance befall him, notice would be taken thereof.

Difcouraged under many difficulties, and in an efpeciall manner tried by the ignorance in which I am day unto day, of my deare *Hufband's* prefent fortune, be it ill or well; pray to be preferved in Faith: if not thus held up, how ofte fhould I have beene difmayed and funke beneath the weight of care and perplexitie.

Aug. 19, Saturday.

This morning, as for feveral paft dayes, awakened contrarie to my wont, with little fenfe of Refrefhment or renewed Strength; ufually the Night bringeth Reft to my wearied frame and Sleepe to mine eyes. *Care-charming Sleepe,* fayth the Poet, *Sweete Father of foft Reft,* as he hath it in another place; but yefter night Sleepe was troubled by the Reftleffneffe of waking Thoughts, like the fwell of the Ocean after the Winds are ftilled: and fo the day, commenced under this Depreffion of Spirit, did feeme onely as another burden, an added day of Tafke-worke to bee performed. Neither received I the fweete renewal of Truft and Hope from my Devotions, that is fo ofte gracioufly permitted mee to enjoy; neverthelefse I was preferved from the prefumptuous Sinne of repining. If for a time the light of

His countenance is withdrawne, who am I, the pooreſt of His Creatures, that I ſhould complaine, if my path, when it ſeemeth to Him good, ſhould bee through the darke valley of Humiliation; ſo I walked ſorrowfully on my way, uncomforted from within or from without; thought on the text, *In thy afflictions He is afflicted, and the Angel of his Preſence ſaveth thee,* but this comfort ſeemed not intended for mee.

1648.

Begin to doubt, that I have beene too readie to bee ſatisfied with myſelf, and to ſay to my ſoule *Peace, peace, where there is no peace,* and have not beene ſo contrite and broken under a ſenſe of Sinne; and ſo is it not unrepented Sinne which doth ſtand betweene mee and the light of my Father's Countenance? Read the 51ſt *Pſalm,* but ſtill felt in Darkneſſe.

Aug. 22, Tueſday.

To night hath *God* ſpoken to mee by the voice of my little Child. It did chaunce that late in the evening I had occaſion to give ſome orders in the Nurſerye, paſſing by the bed I ſtooped to kiſſe my little Girle as I aſked her, had ſhe ſayd her Prayers to Nurſe? She anſwered, No, I ſayd them to *God.* I told her *God* will bleſſe little Children who pray to Him, and he lookes downe and ſees us all. Yes,

1648.

she answered, keeping the whiles fast hold on my apron, *God sees Father in the Ship a long way off, and he sees me in Bed, and when I feel affraid in the darke I say, Please God I am a good little Child sometimes.* *Except ye become as little Children ye cannot enter into the Kingdome of Heaven. Lord, increase my Faith. I believe, helpe thou mine unbeleefe. Why art thou cast downe, O my Soule, and why art thou disquieted within mee? hope thou in God.* Chastened but not without Hope, I goe to my Bed and lay mee downe in Peace, praying to become as a little Child.

Aug. 25, Friday.

Much impressed with a sense of the *Divine* Godnesse towards us, whilest so many are induring all the dreadfull Calamities of Warre at their very doores, than which none have beene brought to such a height of Suffering as the poore besieged People at *Colchester*, for more than two moneths have they held out, till it is sayd the Cries of the starving Women and Children are very great; Numbers are driven to the eating the flesh of Horses and Dogges; and of this now there is little left. One Woman got out of the Towne with her Children to begge from the Parliament Armie, and was driven backe.

Lady Willoughby.

 Now they say many hundreds of Women were let to come out of the Towne, and were then fired upon by Col. *Rainsborough* both with Cannon and Musketts, according to some not loaded with shot, yet would not the Towne let them come backe: what did become of the poore Creatures? Well may Ordinances be passed for dayes of Publicke Humiliation to bewaile the Sinnes of the Nation: yet to what purpose, when they goe on the more sinning, as if they beleeved they could fast and pray away their Sinnes as easily as wash their hands. *Keepe backe thy Servant from presumptuous Sinnes.*

 Heare to day that *Colchester* has surrendered; and that Sir *George L'Isle* & Sir *Charles Lucas* were shot, to retaliate it is sayd the same Crueltie exercised by them in like circumstances.

 Good old Dr. *Sampson* called: he had heard it was reported that the *King* had made his Escape from the *Isle of Wight*.

1648.
Aug. 26,
Saturday.

Sept. 1,
Friday.

Dec. 13,
Wednesday.

From the Diary of

1648-9.

Feb. 3,
Saturday.

1648-9.

Errour and amazement doe fill all Men's minds, so unheard of a Crueltie did seeme impossible, even by the *King's* bitterest Enemies; surely the Judgements of the *Lord* will be drawn down upon this unhappie Countrey. What further Suffering shall bee, wee know not, before the Nation is chastised and purged from its Iniquities. Renewed cause of Thankfulnesse, that my beloved *Husband* did betimes withdraw himself from the Councels of these Men: oft did he use to say to mee, they could on no pretence take the *King's* Life, how little can wee foresee whereunto men's Passion will lead them.

My poore *Fanny* can scarce sleepe at nights, so besett is shee with the Image of the mur-

Lady Willoughby.

thered *King:* when the Newes were told of a sudden, she nigh fainted. *Die's* Griefe hath more of Indignation, and hardly can shee refraine wishing to heare of some signal Vengeance being taken. Gave orders that the Household should put aside and desist from their several Occupations, that the remainder of the Day might be kept with due Solemnitie befitting the sad occasion: at Evening Service all were sensibly affected, at the seasonable Exhortation of the *Chaplaine* on this awfull Event.

Heare with no small concernment that Coll. *Hutchinson* was one of those who did put their Names to the Sentence given against the *King:* one of more honourable repute as a Christian and Gentleman I never heard speake of: wherefore it cannot be doubted but that he hath beleeved himself called upon by his Conscience to this Act, and I would also hope, others likewise have beene constrained to join in it against their naturall feelings, but even Zeale in a good cause requireth to be kept downe by a sober Judgement: so long as the Flame burneth Heaven-ward, it is a pure and shining Light; but turned Earth-ward, it becometh a fierce and destructive Fire.

Letter from my *Sister;* she sayth Proclama-

1648-9.

Feb. 13, *Tuesday.*

1648-9

tion hath been made, that whofoever fhall proclaime another to bee *King*, fhall be put to death as a Traitour.

Fanny, who hath beene ailing of late, was yefter night fo feaverifh that I gave her a compofing Draught, and fhe keeps her bed to day.

Feb. 14, Wednefday.

Fanny better; think to give her a courfe of Bitters: my *Mother* did much recommend them taken fafting every Morning.

March 15, Thurfday.

More Executions; the three Lords have beene beheaded: Lady *Holland* had ceafed not importuning for the *Earl's* life, and buoyed herfelf up with hope to the laft; and when the *High Court* granted a Reprieve for two dayes, fhe and other Ladies and Relatives of the Prifoners had great Expectations there would be a Pardon, and fo was it nearly carried in the *Houfe*: as the Speaker's was the cafting Vote, and he gave it againft him; he having juft before by his Voice in favour of Lord *Goring* faved that bad Man, in regard of fome private Services hee had rendered to him: yet did caufe the Death of one who, though he might have done fome Wrong to his partie, had ever beene a Friend to the Poore and to thofe who were oppreffed and perfecuted for their Religion, and who was civil and courteous to all People. Some particulars were related to mee, by one who is well acquainted with one of my Lrd. *Holland's* Friends who did accompanie him to the Scaffold.

Mr. *Hodges* had much difcourfe with him after his Sentence, being defirous to comfort him. He would not fee his Wife and Children, faying it would adde too much to his Sorrow: he was for a while in great Agonie of minde in that he had not affurance of Pardon for his Sinnes; but it pleafed *God* in his great Mercie to raife him up out of this afflicted condition, and after paffing through a fevere conflict of Spirit, he remained in a cheerefull frame of Minde to the end. He flept foundly the night before his Execution, infomuch he was with fome difficulty awakened; he went to the Scaffold without fhewing any Feare; and fhewed himfelf to the People, who were moved with forrow at the fight of him; he tooke an affectionate leave of his Friends, and fo did fubmit to be put to Death.

It is to mee matter of Amazement as well as of Sorrow, that Men pay fo fmall Regard to the right every man hath to his owne Life, which *God* hath given to him, and which Hee

1649.

March 30, Friday.

April 17, Tuesday.

alone can take away. Vengeance is not for Man, weake and erring; the Promise is given that Evil shall be overcome of Good, not by Evil.

The Time seemeth very long before I can with reason expect to heare from the *Barbadoes*. The *Dutch* Marchant Ships, it is reported in *London*, sailed in February.

Fanny's Health improves. Since she hath had charge of the Still-room, she hath taken a pleasure in the Cultivation of the Plants, and hath enlarged the Herbe Garden. The Lavender slippes have strucke roote, and she hath good stocke of Clove Gilloflowers; a Neighbour hath promised her an excellent Recipe for making a Conserve of these, obtained as a favour from Mr. *Gerard*, the Chirurgian and Botanist, who sayth of it, that it is exceeding cordiall and wonderfully above measure doth comfort the Heart, being eaten now and then.

Her liking for Reading did lead to her over much Studie; I do blame myself for not giving more heed to the effect upon her Health: it seems that her Sister was more sensible in this matter, and did often indeavour to perswade her to leave her Bookes. In small things as

Lady Willoughby.

in greater, so true is it that the right is a straight and narrow way.

1649.

Our Nephews *William* and *Henry* staying with us, good Laddes in the maine; and wee do expect a Visite shortly from my deare Cousin *Margaret de la Fontaine:* wee have not mett since her Marriage.

April 18, Wednesday.

Receipe. The flowers of Lavender picked from the knaps, I meane the blew part and not the huske, mixed with Cinnamon, Nuttmeg, and Cloves, made into Pouder and given to drinke in the distilled Water thereof, prevaileth against Giddinesse. Conserve of the Flowers made with sugar.

April 20, Friday.

This Recipe given to mee by Mr. *Gerard's* Aunte.

Mr. *Gerard* doth recommend for a Cold and Cough, or sore Throate, a Decoction of Hyssope, made with Figges added; or Figges boiled, and Honie and Rue added thereto.

From the Diary of

1651.

May 24,
Saturday.

1651.

His our Wedding day: a sweete morning; rose early: first Thoughts saddened by the absence of him, who is indeed first in my Hearte, but not here to give the welcomings of Love so precious to mee; so sweet to receive and lay up with recollections of other like Endearments to live upon in Absence, preserved, as some one saith, in the Memorie as in a Cabinet richly stored, garnered in Faith, and safely locked with the Key of a loving Constancie: and truly can I say, no Mistrust hath ever fallen upon our deare Affection for each other. Although in looking backe through these sixteene Yeares now past, to the early part of my wedded Life, I do perceave that there was on my part some Constraint and

an over feare of difpleafing, and haply fome Perverfitie of Temper, that made fome things appeare as Unkindneffes that were not fo intended; yet was it I truly beleeve more through Ignorance and the newneffe of my Situation. My deare *Mother* had exercifed fuch a tender Care over me, that like a timid bird no more fheltered by the parent Wing from the rough Winds and pitileffe Storme, I was affrighted, and oft times would faine have returned to the Arke. But the olive Branch appeared above thefe darke Waters, and was found to be a fure Refting Place for the fole of my Foot, and its roots were firmely fixed, and it hath ftood firme. Wee have need of two faiths, faith in humane Affection, and the higher faith, in Divine Wifdome and Love: *Lord, I beleeve, help Thou mine unbeleefe*, is the earneft fupplication of my Hearte. Oh if wee were conftant in this praier, how manie feeble Knees would be ftrengthed, how many hard and rebellious Thoughts be kept downe.

Sixteene yeares ago, I do well remember the morning was like this: the Sunne fhone brightly, and my Sifters did thinke mee happie to be the choice of the brave Lord *Willoughby*; his comelineffe and youth made him to bee

1651.

greatly admired by them, as hee was by manie others. Since that day how much hath come to paſſe: Trouble and Difficulties to overcome not a few: then my firſt Child borne, bringing new hope and a Joy unſpeakable; but the ſweete Bloſſome was early nipped, and the cup of joy daſhed from my lippes: Oh *God*, thou knoweſt what I ſuffered, that my Faith was tried to the uttermoſt, and for a while failed; but Thy Mercie and Truth failed not: Other Children were given to us, lent and gracioufly ſpared: My deare and excellent *Mother* tooke her peacefull departure; this a Sorrow, but not a Sorrow without Hope, no Bitterneſſe was in it; her Worke was ended, and I had no wiſh to keepe her from her Reſt. Precious *Mother!* I humbly hope I have not been infenfible of my privileges: I think I may ſay that under a ſenſe of my owne favoured Lot in this reſpect, I have always felt much tender Solicitude for ſuch as are early deprived of maternal Care, whether knowne or unknowne to mee.

During this long period I have had the Happineſſe of feeing my beloved *Huſband* zealous and active for the Publicke Good, and protected through many Dangers; and though very frequent have beene our Separations, and this laſt the moſt diſtant and perillous; yet have they beene mercifully permitted to his greater Safety. Thus in caſting this backward looke over paſt yeares, I am led to acknowledge with Thankfulneſſe the gracious dealings of our *Heavenly Father* to us, and eſpecially would I note my *Huſband's* timely Withdrawal from a party of Men who have fallen into the Snare ſpread by worldly Pride and Ambition, and in the end brought about the Death of the *King*.

Oft have I beene caſt downe as the Sinne and Suffering, that doe ſo fearefully abound, were from time to time brought before mee; but ſtrength hath beene given mee to endure, and praiſe be unto *Him* who hath vouchſafed a meaſure of Faith, whereby the diſcipline of Life is now viewed in a more cheereful ſpirit, and its burdens and imperfections borne with leſſe of Impatience as Yeares do encreaſe, and I am able more entirely to acknowledge that *the Judgements of the Lord are true and righteous altogether*: and if ſo in mine owne experience, may I not truſt that in Publicke Affaires in like manner, Man's doings are working out the purpoſes of the *Lord* of *Lords* and *King* of *Kings;* that the Nation, when it ſhall have

1651.

passed through this Fire of tribulation and anguish, shall rise up in a newe and righteous Libertie, and bee at Peace.

But little to add this evening to the foregoing: after fervent Supplication for my deare absent Love, went downe stairs and was met by the deare Children, each of them with a Posie of flowers, Cowslips, Primroses, and Hawthorne; and *Fanny* had gathered some of more raritie from her garden. *Die* was eager to know the number of Yeares we have been maried, that she might give directions for the same number of Pies to be made, according to the custome in these Parts, that there should be set on the Table a Pie for every Yeare that a couple have beene maried, and she and her Sister ranne away to order 16 Pies: They are kindly hearted and gladsome creatures, and most dutifull and comforting Children.

July 4, Friday.

Received tidings that the Ship in which my *Husband* did saile, hath reached *Barbadoes*. Thankes be unto the *Lord* who hath brought them unto their desired Haven.

July 7, Monday.

The deare Letter yesternight hath filled my Hearte with Joy and Thankfulnesse.

Lady Willoughby.

1651.
Letter o
Lord
Willoughby,
March 24,
1650.

Moſt Deare Wife,

Wee came to anchor in *Carliſle* Bay, in ſomewhat more than two moneths after we left *Holland*. We fell ſhort of Water, having but halfe a Barrel when wee came in ſight of Land, and were ſtill worſe off for Forrage, and were forced to take the Straw out of the men's cabines, and mix it with ſhavings of Deale boards to give the Horſes to eate. We kept ourſelves concealed ſome dayes, conſidering it the more prudent, till we had all in readineſſe. Wee then appeared in good force and proclaimed the *King*. Numbers joined us, and my Commiſſion met with due reſpect. I ſend this Letter by the Maſter of a Ship ſailing to *London*. Sweete Life and my deare Children, may it fare well with you. During the weariſome Voyage, plans did ſuggeſt themſelves of your joining mee here, but I knowe not how you would endure the hardſhip and dangers of the Paſſage. The Climate of this Iſland is not ſo unhealthy as in ſome others. I hope *Parliament* will not withdraw the Graunt, it would cauſe greate trouble with thoſe who accepted it in Settlement of Demands againſt mee, and might put my deare

1651.

Hearte to inconvenient Straites for Money. Wee are like to have unfriends in both Houſes; it may not bee ſafe to ſay more. Give mee whatſoever Newes of the *King* can be depended on. I cannot beleeve the preſent ſtate of Affaires will laſt long. The heate is greate, nevertheleſſe my Health is good, in the which I do heartily rejoyce, knowing there is One who will be much comforted herein,
Whoſe I am in all
faithfull Affection,
Willoughby.

July 11, Friday.

It is reported, and I feare mee truely, that Sir *George Aſkew* hath ſet ſaile for *Barbadoes*, to take that Iſland and others thereabout from the *King's* Friends. How may I endure the thought that again my beloved *Huſband's* Life is expoſed to all the dangers and ſufferings of Warfare, and this at ſo great diſtance, that for Moneths I ſhall be in ignorance whether he yet live. I thought it well hee ſhould be out of this poore Countrey, full of ſtrife and bloodſhed, but the dangers of Warre are every where.

Sept. 7, Sunday.

Word brought of a Fight at *Worceſter*, and ſome ſay the *Prince* is ſlaine.

Lady Willoughby.

 The rumours that the Prince of *Wales*, or more rightly the *King*, was slaine after the Battaile, not true, though he was wounded in the Hand. He fled from *Worcester*, and it is hoped he hath escaped from his cruell Enemies, as no one knows where he is. A Messenger kindly sent by Mr. *Tobias Bridge*, who setts out for *London* to morrow, and hath engaged to send to my *Husband* a Letter thro' a safe channel by meanes of a Friend of his, a considerable Marchant in the *Citie*, who hath undertaken this out of regard to the Lord *Willoughby*, who did shew some kindnesse to a neare Kinsman of his at the Siege of *Newark*, which he hath not forgotten. Have writt to my *Husband* in such termes as I thought most like to have weight with him that he would yeeld up the Place; telling him, that the most zealous Friends of the *King* do now give up all hope; that his Wife and Children wearie of his absence, and are kept in continual Feare for him; and that as I never had wished to hold him backe from what he judged to bee his duty, so now hee might beleeve that I would not urge him to a course dishonourable, or that would injure others. Likewise I added that all his Friends did agree with me in this opinion.

1651.
Sept. 10.
Wednesday.

1651.

Easier in mind having taken this steppe, so much more hopeful to the Spirit is action, let the thing done towards the desired end be ever so small or by ever so weake a hand, than to remaine, as my lot hath mostly beene, unable to do ought; not even to holde a cup of water to the lippes of him who while I write these Wordes may be lying wounded or dying.

October 31, Friday.

In a Letter from my Sister she sayth, one told her who was present in the *House* when Letters were received from *Paris* containing divers curious Particulars of the *King's* Adventures and Escape. Hee and my Lord *Wilmot* were so sore pushed that on the second day's march from *Worster* they betooke themselves into the Woods, and did sleepe two nights in a Tree, and whilest there some Souldiers came close by, but saw them not. Hee had other marvellous Escapes; and owed his Safetie to a Gentlewoman who disguised him; she cut off his Haire, and put Serving Man's clothes on him, and a Perriwig (hereat, as this curious historie was read aloud, some of the Members refrained not from laughing), he was mounted on a Horse, and she did ride behind him on a Pillion. That which does seeme most wonderfull, the *King* was in *London,* and walked about

Lady Willoughby.

1651.

dreſſed in a Gentleman's habite, and did even look into *Weſtminſter Hall*. The Lord *Wilmot* at length did procure a Marchant Ship; and the *King* followed him into a Houſe, when to their great terrour the Maſter of the Veſſel came to them and ſayd he knew the *King*. They prevailed with Money and Promiſes, and ſailed for *Harvre de Gras*. This Relation did ſeeme ſo full of wonder and mercy towards the poore young *King*, who doubtleſſe would have beene ſlaine had he beene taken, that I have thought it well to copie the ſame from my Siſter's Letter.

Dec. 11, *Thurſday*.

Death of Colonel *Ireton* is much lamented: he did compaſſionate the deplorable condition and miſeries of the People of *Ireland;* and in this barbarous Warfare ſhewed more Mercie than ſome others.

From the Diary of

1651-2.

1651-2.

January 6,
Tuesday.

Ewes sent mee that Letters have beene received by the *House* that Sir *George Afcue* had reduced the *Barbadoes*: and likewife there was read a Copie of an Act of the Lord *Willoughby* and the Affembly, for fequeftring Eftates. This will, I feare mee, inflame people's mindes the more againft him.

Feb. 21,
Saturday.

My Lord *Say* and *Seale* hath fent mee fuch particulars as have come to hand. Sir *George* had taken many Ships, and fired at the Caftell; and they in the Caftell fhot at him and killed one man. Then he fent a Summons to the Lord *Willoughby*, who made anfwer that hee would keepe the place for the *King*, who he was informed was neare *London*, and that all the Countrey came in to him: this it is fuppofed he had beene told by the *Dutch*. Offers were

made of Indemnitie, and great perfuafion ufed
to bring over the People to the *Parliament*.
It was expected that Sir *George Afcue* would
waite fome dayes, in the hope that the *Ifland*
would furrender, before he attempted to land
his Forces.

Alas! I know its brave *Governour* too well
to doubt what courfe hee will take. May the
Lord have mercie upon us, nothing is there for
mee to doe but to keepe neare to the everlafting
Arme that can fupport the weakeft of his creatures, and fave in the midft of the greateft
Dangers.

Mifs the faithfull overfight of *Alice*, tho' of
late fhe had beene too infirme to do much. My
Brother *William* and his Familie make us a large
Houfehold: and to keepe a well ordered and
well provided Houfe is no fmall charge. Since
my Brother compounds for the Eftates, I am
releeved from fome perplexitie. Poore old
Alice, her Death was timely, had fhe lived to
heare of the Execution of the *King*, it would
have gone farre to breake her hearte.

The Diurnal doth containe the report that
Sir *George Afcue* hath taken *Barbadoes*.

Eclipfe of the Sunne: many have been
infected with feare of fome greate Calamitie or

Disturbance to happen at this time, and would not goe out to their Worke, or leave their Houses: the darkness was so great one could not see to reade a booke without the light of a Candle.

No Tydings of my deare *Husband:* and my very Soule is sicke with waiting and listening to catch the lightest Rumour.

My Friends have sent mee all the Information they could obtaine; and my hearte is bowed downe with Thankfulnesse for the mercifull and wonderfull Preservation of that precious *Life*, the object of daily prayer and supplication. It doth appear that my *Lord* did refuse to submit to the Summons of Surrender thrice demanded by Sir *George Ascue*, who thereupon did land some Troopes: the Lord *Willoughby* made a gallant Defence, but by reason of the Darknesse, they thought the Enemie were in number more than they were, and the Seamen running up with great shouts, they were so amazed they gave way: the *Parliament* Forces pursued them to *Fort Royal*, which they stormed, and were joined by Colonel *Muddiford* and his Friends; following this Example, they did engage to live or die with the *Parliament*. The Lord *Willoughby* finding this, marched up to them with all the Force he could make; and whileſt that he held a Councell of Warre, one of the Enemies great Gunnes ſhot in at the doore and carried away the Sentinell's head. A Treatie has beene concluded, Protection being granted to the Lord *Willoughby*, Colonel *Walrund*, and divers others for the keeping their Eſtates in *England* or elſewhere. Surely I may hope to have a Letter ſhortly. Choſe out for my portion of *Scripture* the 103d *Pſalm*. What ſhall I render to the Lord for all his benefits, this crowning Mercie wherewith he hath bleſſed mee?

To-day I had the great happineſſe of a Letter. My deare *Huſband* beareth bravely his ill Fortunes: he was entreated very courteouſly by Sir *George*. My *Lord* doth purpoſe returning by one of his owne Veſſels, having Buſineſſe to ſettle in *Surinam*, and in *Antigua*.

Wingfield tells mee he has had ſome Newes of the Horſe that was ſtolen laſt weeke, and would go to *Ipſwich* to-morrow, that being Market day; told him not to be ſparing of Reward on this occaſion, I would ill like him to be loſt: Bade *Wingfield* ſee at the Weavers when the Linnen would be readie, alſo if the Flax was arrived.

1652.

April 8, Thurſday.

April 9, Friday.

1652.
May 5,
Wednesday.

The Packman is long in coming his rounds, and my waiting woman is alarmed that her ſtores of houſewiferie will ſcarce hold out; and *Fanny* is like to want imbroidery Silks, and doth watch his coming with impatience, as ſometimes he doth bring of Bookes a few ſortes, and Ballads, which ſhe doth eagerly catch up; & he had entered into ſome promiſe of bringing for her a booke of Poems by a Mr. *John Milton*, one that keepes a Schoole at *London*, the ſame it is ſayd, who did write the *Image Breaker*, a Booke that did excite the Indignation of manie; that a man of parts and learning ſhould deſire to injure the memorie of one not onely a Martyr, but who had manie rare qualities, and was our anointed *King*, albeit in that capacitie he did ſome great Wrongs. The worke was little read, the while the ſubject of his attack, the *Eikon Baſilike*, did excite in people ſuch true Sympathie, that it was read with Teares. A Friend did procure one for mee, which not onely doth ſerve to cheriſh a ſorrowful remembrance of the heavy Trial and the Griefes of his late *Majeſty*, but by the pietie and meekneſſe of the ſeveral Meditations, doth greatly tend to Edification and Improvement.

Lady Willoughby.

No Tydings of the old Horſe to be heard at *Ipſwich*: *Wingfield* and one of the men are gone in another direction, ſome miles on the *Loweſtoffe* Road.

1652.
May 7,
Friday.

The men returned this forenoon after two Dayes abſence, bringing with them the poore Animal, jaded and half ſtarved; hope he will looke in better condition before my *Lord's* return. A Man living at *Saxmundham*, who had ſerved in one of his Regiments, had ſeene the Horſe go through the Village, and knew it againe, and by this Clue they traced him.

May 11,
Tueſday.

Lizzy hath finiſhed her Sampler; her Siſter *Die* hath much credit for the ſame, for the Patience with which ſhee hath taught her this, and other Needle-worke.

May 12,
Wedneſday.

Reading our uſual portion of *Holy Scripture* this morning, after ſome Remarks thereon, I felt encouraged to ſay a few wordes to my Daughter *Fanny*. Shee hath leſſe of ſelf-will and heate of temper needing reſtraint and watchfulneſſe than her elder *Siſter*, but falleth into Errour of another ſorte, ſeeming too well inclined to take her eaſe, and ſheweth an in-differency to ſuch Purſuits as ſuite not her Fancie, yet which are of good account and Service in a Familie. Eſpecially ſhe hath of late againe addicted herself over-much to her Bookes, which, if not to the hurt of her Health as formerly was the case, causeth her to bee so enrapt in them, and in the indulgence of her own Imaginations, that she neglecteth those small occasions wherein she might bee of Use or Pleasure to others, and at the same time secure Benefite to herself by being drawne into little acts of Courtesie and Kindnesse, which doe keepe alive and enlarge the kindly Dispositions of our nature, and doubtlesse are soe intended by *Him* who hath planted mankind in Families. She did receeve with meekenesse this Reproof, acknowledging her sometime Negligence, and her Temptation to the unprofitable spending of her Time in some particulars, and did confesse that haply her Affections had beene too highly sett on works of the Fancy and Imagination; although shee sayd, they were such as for the most part did containe manie pious and vertuous Meditations, and added with modesty, that she believed the Minde was elevated and refreshed by drinking at these Fountaines. The while she spoke, raising timidly her eyes & blushing, as she pleaded for some Poets above others, more especially Mr. *Edmund Spenser*, one who hath indeed tuned his Lyre to the utterance of moſt ſweet Truths and deepe Philoſophie, ſhe ſeemed not unaptly deſcribed in his own Wordes:

Ne in her Speech, ne in her 'Haviour,
Was lightneſſe ſeene, or looſe Vainitie,
But gracious Womanhood and Gravitie
Above the reaſon of her youthly yeares.

I can truly ſay it is my deſire, not through an over-ſtrictneſſe or miſconſtruction to narrow the benevolent deſigns of the *Creator* toward his Creatures; hee, with bountifull Hand hath adorned the Heaven and the Earth with beautie, and if he hath in a peculiar manner fitted ſome Mindes to taſte hereof, and to approach him by theſe ways of Pleaſantneſſe & Peace, doubtleſſe it may bee to the attainment of the higheſt *Wiſdome*. Yet, like all things elſe in this World, hath it not its peculiar temptations, this keene Senſe of the Beautifull and aptitude in the diſcernment thereof? doth it not ſometimes lead to a turning away from the rigid aſpect of Dutie, and miniſter to ſelf-gratification under a faire diſguiſement, which maketh it unſuſpected of evill. The Beautifull Gate of the Temple inviteth us to enter, but if ſo be

1652.

wee remaine at the portall, we prophane its sacred purpose.

Once more the *Poet* cometh to my aide.

The meanes therefore which unto us is lent
Him to behold, is on his Workes to looke,
Which hee hath made in beautie excellent;
And in the same, as in a Brazen Booke,
To reade inregistered in every nooke
  His Goodness, which His Beautie doth declare,
  For all that's good, is beautiful and faire.

Through whatsoever ways we are led, how various soever may bee our Gifts, there is but one end, that we may all be brought to see the Beautie of Holinesse, to perceave the Harmonie that doth exist in the morall government of *God*, as in the visible wonders and beauties of Creation, and so come to worship Him in Spirit and in Truth.

May 15, Saturday.

There is like to be a poore Hay harvest, no Raine as yet; this long drought is a great concerne to *Fan*. Some of the Seeds she hath sowne, scarce to be seene; what is more serious, fodder for the cattell is difficult to be had.

May 28, Friday.

Great tempests during the Weeke; raine and winde, and lightening; the Thunder ceased not for houres together. About *London* it is ſaid there were Haile ſtones which did meaſure ſome inches round, and ſome of ſingular ſhape. Much Glaſſe hath been broken.

    Went to ſee *Cicely*, ſhee and her Children are bravely. She had beene to *Langham*, neare unto *Colcheſter*, to viſite her huſband's Mother, whom ſhe did find in a diſtreſſefull ſtate ; her Sonne not well of his wounds, and ſhee, every time ſhe dreſſeth his arme, hearte-broken to thinke that hand had given his *Brother* his death ſtroke. He knew not who it was, till he got ſight of his face as he dropped ; and as he fell on his knees beſide him, he received a Blow on his head, which ſtunned him. This chanced well for him, as he thereby could remaine, he dragged the Bodie of his *Brother* to the ſide of a Hedge, and then as he did paſſionately bewaile his Death, and kiſſed the bleeding Face, he found Life not utterly departed, and ran ſome diſtance to a Ditch where was water, and pouring it into the Laddes mouth, for it was his youngeſt *Brother*, and very deare unto him, he opened his Eyes, and ſeemed to know him, but was paſt Speech, and could onely draw him cloſer, and ſo died. All the Countrey round there was Want and Sickneſſe, the

From the Diary of

1652.

July 10. Saturday.

Grant from the *Parliament* is a seasonable help; but it mendeth not broken bones, nor bringeth backe *Sonnes* and *Husbands* to Life.

For some Weekes I have not left my Chamber, and have beene confined to my Bed the greater part of that time, having beene seised of a sudden Sicknesse; at least so it did then appeare, though continuall harassment & suspence had brought mee into a weakely state for some time past. It happened that some Noise, and the sound of unaccustomed Voices in the Hall, did startle mee for a moment with the notion that my deare *Husband* had come into the House: I hasted downe staires, and some great Packages strucke my Sight, and did the more confirme my Hopes, but it proved only to bee some goods shipp'd from *London*, which had come there by a Marchant Ship from *Barbadoes*. As I turned backe, the shocke of the Disappointment following quicke on the Joy that had seemed so neare, overcame mee, and my Limbes trembled under mee, and I scarce could reach my Roome, and that night a Feaver came on, with such violent Shiverings that I greatly feared it was the Ague. For many Weekes tooke no nourishment but Sage possets, my drinke Whey. Still but poorly.

My deare Children have beene tender Nurſes, and, when I began to recover, yet remaining weake, ſo that I moſtly could beare but one Perſon at a time, I had oftentimes ſweet converſe with Each, and miniſtred to the ſeverall wants of their Characters, as I was favoured with Help ſo to do; endeavouring to impreſs upon them Faithfulneſſe to their Convictions, whether in ſmall things or greate, as the only way to obtaine true Peace.

Alſo hath it beene a ſeaſon of Self-examination, and deepe ſearching of Hearte; and my Birthday happening when I was thus layd low, I endeavoured to paſſe it profitably, and to queſtion myſelf if, as I approched nearer and nearer to the Grave, I was the nearer Heaven. Selfe ſeemed the great Hinderance in the way of improvement. It is a hidden Idolatrie and often unſuſpected. Is it not Selfe that prevents our eye beeing ſingle?

Read ſome portion of the *Scriptures* that were not ſo familiar to mee as other, or as they ſhould bee.

I would here note downe, as a cauſe of Thankfulneſſe, one of a multitude of tender mercies and loving kindneſſes of my *Heavenly Father*, his raiſing mee up and reſtoring mee

1652.

July 12, *Monday.*

1652.

to Health, and to the care of my deare Children in their Father's abfence; and alfo that with returning Health he hath given mee a rejoycing Hearte. As I walked forth in the warme Sunne fhine, the Fragrancie of the Aire, and every thing around mee fo full of Beautie, it did feeme that truly *My Youth was renewed like the Eagles*, fo fweet and pleafant were my Thoughts.

July 12, Monday.

To-day my Strength was fo farre increafed that I was able to walke downe to the Brooke, and fate downe on the warme funnie Banke.

From the *Queft of Cynthia*, by Michael Drayton. Ed.

The Winds were hufht, no Leafe fo fmall
 At all was feene to ftirre,
Whileft tuning to the Water's fall
 The fmall Birds fang to her.

Thought of my deare and honoured *Mother*, and of the laft time wee did paffe together at this Spot; the little Streame of cleere water did now run gurgling on juft as it did then, and the Flowers and the moffie Banke were there, but my *Mother's* voice no more, yet did fhe feeme neare mee, and nearer in this, that fome of her experience had now beene mine, Sorrow and Death had beene my teachers,

Ministers of his that do his pleasure; but he leaveth not his Children comfortlesse: the words of the *Lord Jesus* sustained mee, His Life and His Death were my Strength and Consolation. How sweet is it, that the Memorie of my *Mother* is ever linked with peaceful and holie Thoughts. Oh might I so live that my deare *Children* might so thinke of mee, but I am not worthie of this. Oh that the desire may bee more present with mee, and put more of Heaven into my Love for them. I do confesse, with sorrow and contrition of Hearte, that my Solicitude for them hath beene more Worldly as they have growen older, and the fence of their immortall Destination not so abiding, as when they were younger, Gifts newly from *God's* owne Hand, and Talents entrusted to my Stewardship.

Yester-noone, Thankes bee unto the *Most High,* to my unspeakable joy and comfort my deare Life returned to his Familie, through Mercie well in Health, but changed by the long Sea-voyages and the climate of the *Indies;* this, though onely in the outward, beeing the same loving *Husband* and *Father.* He stayed not in *London;* but so soone as he could leave the Ship, did earnestly set forth hitherward.

1652.

July 19, Monday.

He expresseth some surprise to find the Nation so quiet, the joy of our Meeting was saddened by the manie relations to be given of the Murther of the late *King* and of some of his former Friends, and divers other particulars of the state of Affaires and Parties, and the hopelesse condition of his present *Majestie*; of familie Newes there was much to learne. Mr. *Edmund Spenser* sayth,

> One loving Houre
> For manie Yeares of sorrow can dispense,
> A dram of Sweet is worth a pound of Soure;
> She hath forgot how manie a wofull stoure,
> For him she hath endured: She speaks no more
> Of past; true is, that true Love hath no power
> To looken backe; his Eyes bee fixed before.

Feare that I can scarce say this, not having so great Hopefulnesse.

    My deare Life is well satisfied with his Daughters, and knoweth not which he doth the most admire; yet methought his eye turned to the youngest most lovingly; he is pleased to commend my Care of them. I had feares that he might thinke them forward, or deficient in observance of some ceremonies, and did assay some little Apologie, if they were more free in his presence than did seeme altogether becomming, seeing they had beene, in consequence of my retired Life, more with mee than is customarie. In my lonely State I was faine to solace myselfe with their sweet Societie, and did encourage them to feele unrestrained before mee; manie a lonesome and wearie Houre have they lightened by their simple Talke, and eased mee not seldom of troubled thoughts by their dutifull Affection.

He smiled as he replied he knew not what might be deemed too forward, they spake not to him without Blushing, yet were they free from awkward Bashfulnesse, he wished them none otherwise, or in aught different, and had onely to desire that they might grow up such as their Mother. Teares did spring to my Eyes as he uttered these kind Words; but although as a Wife the prayse was sweet and incouraging, and I beleeve might be so received without conceit, yet in my Hearte did arise the secret Prayer, that they might be much better Women than their Mother. He added, no Father could desire better or prettyer Children, and in his absence *Diana* had so grown, she was, tho' not so handsome as *Fanny*, an exceed-

1652.

July 27, Tuesday.

ing lovely young Creature. *So we are rich in our Daughters, if in nought elfe.*

This Evening my *Lord* difcourfed fome time on his feverall Adventures, affording us fome pleafing entertainment by his Hiftorie of the different Iflands and Places; already is there a Towne, which he has called *Parham,* began building on the north of the Ifland of *Antigua;* and on the Southern fide of the fame Ifland a beautiful Bay, into the which he failed, and found fhelter from a Storme, which fuddenly arofe, and as it was through the following his Councell that they fteered in this courfe, it was named by the Sailers *Willoughby Bay;* and hence has beene fo called by others, fo our name, and that of our deare *Parham* may abide, and may fome day be familiar words to the Voyager, and amidft a ftrange People, when our Race may be paffed away, and the place thereof be knowne no more.

Aug. 4, Wednefday.

My *Lord* having fixed on our Departure for *London,* have beene too bufie to take up the Penne. Hee could not beare to leave his Familie fo fhortly after his Returne; alfo to mee the feparation would have beene ill to beare, now that I have againe enjoyed the fupport and happinesse of his Presence, so it is determined that wee take Lodgings and remaine at *London* the while our Affaires may make it needful so to doe.

Came to our Lodgings, which are conveniently situated in *Russel Street, Covent Garden.*

My Sister called and tooke us in her Coach to the *Parke.* As wee passed *Whitehall* wee alighted, and did looke with Awe and Sadnesse on the scene of his late *Majestie's* Death. The place through which hee was taken on to the Scaffold having beene newly bricked up, points out the exact Spot. The Girls wished to enter the *Palace*, but there were no meanes at hand, neither could I be sure it would be prudent.

This day went to *Northumberland House;* there informed that Lady *Lisle* was in a dangerous state, shee had beene doing well till yester night; the Babie is a healthy Child.

Mett the Earle of *Winchelsea* at *Spring Gardens*, he joined us; he seemeth a Man of some Sence, and hath a lively and polite Manner.

Heard the sorrowfull newes of Lady *Lisle's* Death. The Bodie is to bee carried downe to *Penshurst* for Interment. Mr. *Algernon Sydney* doth accompanie thither his afflicted Brother.

1652.

Aug. 10,
Tuesday.

Aug. 12,
Thursday.

Aug. 13,
Friday.

1652.

Aug. 18,
Wednesday.

Auguſt 22,
Sunday.

Auguſt 23,
Monday.

It is thought my Lord *Leiceſter* will be likely to keepe the Children at *Penſhurſt*.

Mr. *John Evelyn* called, the Lord *Say*, and others.

Went to heare Mr. *Owen* preach in the morning; in the evening heard Dr. *Jeremy Taylor*.

Went forth early in the Day; returning from *Weſtminſter* wee tooke a Boate at *Whitehall*, a landing place runs out ſome way into the River, and the Boats are brought up cloſe to the ſide, ſo that to ſome it was an eaſie matter to ſtep in, and thoſe accuſtomed to this, had no more feare or difficultie than in ſtepping into a Coach; for myſelfe, I doe confeſſe it ſeemed of no eaſie accompliſhment: the Boat appeared narrow, though, wee were told, it was one of the largeſt ſize in common uſe. It had a convenient Shade or awning, with Windowes, and was pulled by ſix Rowers. Wee went at an amazing rate; and it did ſeeme marvellous how wee avoided running againſt other Boats, or they againſt us. Landed at the *Tower Staires*, could ſcarce beleeve it ſafe for my *Lord* to be walking ſo neare this darke Priſon-houſe, but could not prevaile with him to haſten his ſteps, hee deſiring to ſhew to his

Lady Willoughby.

Children as much as he could fee to point out of his former Prifon. "Who next will be murthered there?" he whifpered; I fhuddered to heare him fpeake of the Lords *Capel* and *Holland*, afking mee of the manner of their Death, and how it was taken by the People, and other Queftions, all moft untimely, to my thinking.

Begin to wearie of this great Towne; fo much going hither and thither. Our Kinfman, Mr. *Willoughby*, called to-day, and tooke us to the *Royall Exchange:* it is a Quadrangle, and hath a Piazza round each fide, within are benches for people to reft upon. Above this covered walke there are Shops containing rich Marchandife from the *Indies*, both Eaft and Weft, and elfewhere; Haberdafhers' fhops, and others of divers kindes.

The Earle of *Winchelfea* hath appeared to affect our Societie more than our flight acquaintance did feeme to neceffitate, the reafon whereof is now made to appeare.

Retired early this evening, a Subject of much Solicitude having beene brought before my Minde, and truly one very unexpected. The Earle of *Winchelfea* hath expreffed his defire to allie himfelfe with our Familie, having fixed

1652.

Auguft 28, *Saturday.*

Sept. 20, *Monday.*

1652.

his Affections on my deare Daughter *Diana*, and doth crave Permiffion to waite upon her, and expreffeth his humble hope, that wee will looke favorably on his fuite. Our knowledge of him is but fmall; but I have heard my *Mother* fpeake of his Familie, fhee having had great efteeme for this Earle's Grandmother, with whom fhee had good acquaintance, & did confider herfelfe honoured thereby. When Lady *Maidftone*, fhee received the Title of Counteffe of *Winchelfea* from the hands of his late *Majeftie;* and this in refpect of her worth and great merits, fhee having beene previoufly raifed to the Peerage by *King James*: So that my Lord *Winchelfea* cometh of good Parentage, a matter not to be lightly confidered. It would doubtleffe bee a fatisfaction to beftow our Daughter on one come of a good Lineage, and who in other refpects feemeth deferving of regard; neverthleffe my Minde is impreffed with a painfull Senfe of the uncertaintie how farre this Connexion may bee for her true happineffe, and with the certaintie that Trialls of manie forts attend this change of condition. The fharpeft Paines and Sorrowes of life are infeparable from its brighteft Joys. It is like unto bidding my deare Child *God* fpeed, on her setting forth on a long and hazardous Voyage to an unknowne Country beyond my helpe, and expofed to divers hidden Dangers, and haply even Death. Who knoweth what a day may bring forth? the early morning may shine out brightly; but soone doe the clouds arise and obscure its brightnesse; and oft the bow of promise, discerned through the falling Raine, is the onely token of future Sunneshine; so is Life: but for the gracious Promises made visible to the eye of Faith, a darke and troublous passage, a discipline whereby the will is to bee subjugated and Selfe sacrificed, and so the Heart purified: what sayeth the Prophet: *Hee shall sit as a refiner of silver.* So wee must bee tried, even by fire, till our corrupt Nature is fitted to receive the Divine Image. But though I am prone to consider Life, perhaps, under too gloomie an Aspect, as beeing more alive to the suffering of the Conflict, than to the peace of Victorie, yet have I through Infinite Mercie beene sustained under Temptation and Triall; and should not I have the same trust for this deare Child. Also I have received great earthly comfort and delight in the endeared relations of Wife and Mother, and the same may bee her experience, and

1652.

haply through lesse inward conflict: shee hath a cheereful and brave Spirrit, and a loving and good Heart, and is worthie the esteeme and love of any Man. How great a Comfort and Joy she hath beene to mee, and this in especiall manner during the past two Yeares, when she hath greatly indeared herselfe to mee by her Thoughtfulnesse and Readinesse to helpe and cheere mee when all other outward Support failed: this may not be told, nor at this time should it bee too keenely remembered.

October 5, Tuesday.

Calls from our Kinsfolke and Friends: The Earle introduced his Sister *Lady Waller*.

October 6, Wednesday.

Mr. *John Evelyn* called, and wee returned with him to *Sayes Court*. Tooke a Boate to *Deptford*: Went over the Garden to looke at the improvements therein: He doth say it can never be to him so sweet a place as *Wotton*; still he bestoweth time and paines, and hath much pleasure in laying out walkes, planting, and so forth. We were shewen manie Curiosities, Bookes, Pictures and the like; the dried Plants pleased *Fanny*.

Little time for Reading or quiet Meditation. Went to see the *Portugal* Ambassador goe in state to the *Parliament House*.

October 23, Saturday.

The *Earle* importunes for an early Day;

my *Husband* inclines to the fame for divers reafons. Although there appeareth a Settlement of the Nation, and an outward Quietneffe and Submiffion of Parties, fome there bee who are unwilling to fuppofe it will laft, and hints are occafionally dropped among Friends, of fecret Letters and Miffions; and this Mariage would put one of our Familie, as my *Lord* doth expreffe it, to faile in another Boate.

From the Diary of

1653.

April 5, Tuesday.

1653.

A Sad Mischance hath befallen the tame Redbreast, which had not beene seene for neare a Weeke, & wee supposed it had a Nest which kept it away; but it hath beene found lying neare the Windore of the Apple-roome, not much used of late, starved to death. *Diana* will lament to heare the sad fate of the little Bird shee did feed all the Winter, which was so tame hee would pecke out of her Hand. The old Raven too hath dyed since shee went away.

From the Countess of *Winchelsea* to the Ladie *Willoughby*.

Madame,

Your Ladyship's Letter was duly received by mee, and hath given mee Comfort. Deare *Mother*, I will strive to walke after the excellent advice you give mee: this great Citie is exceeding lonesome; I will do my endeavour to thinke lesse of the Fields and Woods of *Parham*. My Heart pineth for Home, and meethinks one Kisse from my *Mother* would bee a Consolation, and leave mee to more contented thoughts; but I desire not to complaine, neither have I just cause. The *Earle* speakes of our going into *Rutlandshire* this Summer: *Burleigh*, I heard saye, is a fine place. We went to suppe at Mr. *Pepys'*, and heard an *Italian* Musician plaie on a Harpe in an astonishing manner: Mr. *Evelyn* was there, hee did inquire concerning your health and of my Sister *Fanny*, who, I do assure you, hee doth admire greatly; hee sayth people of fashion doe now beginne the Yeare as doe Foreiners, in *Januarye*, the change is like to bee troublesome; some one made the remarke that the Spring time seemeth more properly to begin the yeare than the Winter, and so it seemeth to mee.

Deare *Mother*, I hope this will find you in Health; also my honoured *Father*, to whom is my dutifull Affection: I desire my Love to my Sisters, and hoping you will excuse

this poore writing, as you know I did never excell in this Arte, I remaine
Your Ladyſhip's obedient
and loving Daughter,
D. *Winchelſea.*

Strand,
6*th of April,* 1653.

Madame,

The *Earle* doth informe mee that a Meſſenger is going Northward, and hath offred mee, if I wiſhed to write to your Ladyſhip, hee would ſend my Letter. Though but little diſpoſed I take up the penne: I cannot ſend you the better account of my Health you ſo much deſire to heare; and at times, deareſt *Mother,* I am ſo low, I wonder almoſt if I am the ſame Creature that was once merrie enough. Yeſter-day in the forenoone I rode out by the *Earle's* deſire in the new Coach: he hath taken great paines in the ordering of it; it is made after the patterne that Mr. *Evelyn* brought from *Paris;* wee were nigh beeing upſet in *Drury Lane,* by reaſon of the deepe tracks into which the wheels ſanke, and a Wagon load of Hay mett us; after a deale of lifting and pufhing, wee went on. The fweet fcent of the Hay coming in at the windore tooke my thoughts to *Parham*, and to thofe dayes when I was happier riding with *Fanny* and little *Befs* in our Hay-cart, than fitting ftately up in this fine Coach. Rode in *Hide Parke*; they paie one fhilling now at the Gate, which difpleafes manie. On Wednefday, in *Mulberie Gardens*, met Mr. *Evelyn* and Mrs. *Evelyn*, and fome Ladies: here were a number of gaily dreffed Perfons, and Tables of refrefhment.

    Hoping you are well,
     deare *Mother*,
  I reft your Ladyfhip's moft
    obedient & loving Daughter,
      D. *Winchelfea*.

Strand,
16th of *July*, 1653.

 P.S. My *Lord* tells mee your Ladyfhips old friend Sir *Harry Vane* hath taken the late conduct of the *Protector* fo ill, that hee hath retired to *Raby Caftell*.

Have heard no Newes of my Daughter *Winchelfea* for fome time, to-day did receive a Letter writt with Cheerfulneffe and in good

October 25, Tuefday.

1653.

Hearte at the Prospect before her; *The Lord hear her in the day of trouble.* It is a triall not to bee with her at a time when no person can bee the comfort which I know that I should bee to my deare Child; but wee must submit: shee will have kind Friends and good care I doubt not. Shee hath beene at the Christening at *Sayes Court*, and findeth herselfe in no way the worser, but indeed the better, for the lively Companie shee did there meete. Good Mr. *Owen* did perform the Service in Mr. *Evelyn's* Librarie; this I thinke is Mr. *Evelyn's* second Sonne.

October 27, Thursday.

To-day read in 1 *Corinthians*, 13 Chap. 4. Verse. Under a trying sence of Discouragement in the failure of an endeavour to set some Affaires straight which did concerne others as well as myselfe, wherein one shewed a Jealousy and meane Suspicion very grievous to mee: I sate downe in my chamber, moved to teares at this Unkindenesse in one from whom I did expect farre otherwyse. In this Despondency, and lett mee confesse it, not without some feelings of Resentment, the wordes of the Text were brought before mee, *Charitie suffereth long, vaunteth not itselfe, is not puffed up:* Felt humbled; had I not shewen an impatience of

Temper, a readineſſe to take Offence, and to juſtifie myſelfe? *Is not puffed up;* Had I not given inçouragement to a ſelfe-ſatisfied Spirrit, like the *Phariſee*, that I was not as other Men are, and ſo was guiltie of a worſe Fault than hee whom I did condemne? Spirituall Pride beeing the worſt ſort of Pride: now after that my perturbation had ceaſed, and through a little wholeſome ſelfe-examination, I did ſtrive to overcome vaine Thoughts of myſelfe and evil Thoughts of another, ſome parte of the Buſineſſe did appeare in a new light, and ſhortly afterward I was able to convince my Friend, who did immediately repent him of the termes he had uſed. It is not enough alwayes to bee in the right, but wee muſt bee carefull not to obſcure the Truth by too greate anxietie to make others thinke wee are.

From the Diary of

1654.

April 22, Saturday.

1654.

His afternoone arrived my *Daughter Winchelſea* and her Infant, Servants, &c. A Coach drawne by ſix Horſes was a ſight in *Parham*, and all the Village ranne out, and manie People collected at the Gate, ſome for the ſight, others to teſtifie their pleaſure: *Nurſe* had come up to the Houſe, likewiſe *Cicely* and her Children, and the Hall was crowded with faces when my deare Child entered once more her *Father's* Houſe.

Never was a greater rejoycing in our Houſehold. As I remained with *Die* for ſhort ſpace in the Parlour, and looked in her ſweet face enquiringly, teares ſtarted to her eyes, but momentarie, her preſent Joy ſhone through them, and ſaying, I am happie now, my *Mother*, ſhee quickly ledde me up to the

Nurferie to fee her Child; as wee did enter the roome, fuch a din of voices fcared the poore little Fellow, and hee was juft fetting up a diftreffefull crie when hee caught fight of his *Mother's* Face, and was pacified: Nurfe rubbed her Spectacles, and could not enough admire him. Quietnefs in the Houfe at laft. At night feelings were revived of paft Sorrow; as I ftood with my *Daughter* by the Cradle where her little *Sonne* was fleeping, the fame in which my *Firft-borne* had once flept, in the full promife of Health and Life; yet fo foone to lie there in the fleepe of Death.

The beft Bed-roome had beene made readie with no fmall preparation of the Toylet Table, the new white Satin Pinnecufhion imbroidered by *Fanny;* the chafed Silver Candleftickes given mee by my *Uncle;* the rofe-coloured Ewers of Venetian Glaffe Silver mounted; and the Cup and Stand of wrought Gold fet with ftones, brought by my *Father* from the *Netherlands;* and *India* boxes for pouders and perfumes. Two *Maids* were in attendance, and *Nurfe* ftood at the Doore dreffed in her beft Gowne and Apron of fine Lawne, and her white Cap and Kercher, to receive the young Counteffe, who did laugh merrily at all this

1654.

April 28, Friday.

state; and afterward, when wee did parte for the night, as fhe did looke around her, and at the high Bed, the thicke Dammafke Curtaines, and fpread with a rich Coverlet of quilted Satin, fhee prayed fhee might be permitted after this night to fleepe with her Sifter in their old pleafant Chamber.

Have fetled to our accuftomed Wayes, excepting that there is ever a going to and fro to the Nurferie, and young Mafter calleth out Luftily. He is furely a fine *Child:* Our Neighbours are fomewhat furprized that my *Daughter* taketh on herfelfe not more Sedateneffe or Ceremonie. True is it that when her Prefence is required fhee is feldome to be found in the withdrawing Roome; yefterday, in the afternoone, when Companie did arrive, fhee was downe at the *Dairie* making acquaintance with her pet Calfe *Strawberrie,* now growne up into a fine brindled Cow: In the Still-roome with her Sifter, her fweet merrie voice is like my little *Die* of yeares paft; but when at worke with mee, fhee fometimes falleth into a fadder Mood, yet it paffeth away. It pleafeth mee to fee her enjoy her dear Sifters companie and the Occupations of the Countrey, but fhee doth feeme more indifferent to the Abfence of the *Earle* than I would shee did; I have adventured discreetly to approch the subject, but shee doth dextrously avoide saying ought that should imply Discontentment on her part, or Unkindnesse or Dissatisfaction on her *Husband's*; and I have heard from others, that the Match was acceptable to his Kindred, who have severally shewen their esteeme for her. If any Cause there bee of a Personall kind, in the Temper or Habits that giveth her Uneasinesse, which standeth in the way of a more entire Affection toward him who should be first in her Honour and Love, she keepeth it to herselfe: hard, yea, and unbearable must bee the Yoke, and bitter the Bondage, where Love is not, or but a divided Affection; and woe is mee, I have great feares for my *Child's* Happinesse, and in this Trouble I can do little or nothing to lighten her Burthen. *The Heart knoweth its owne Bitternesse, and a Stranger intermeddleth not.* It is so farre well that there doth exist no want of outward Courtesie or Respect in my Lord *Winchelsea's* Deportment. Hee is much in the gaie World, and as some Men affect an indifferency toward their Wives as more dignified, if such bee the present Mode his is not the Minde to contemne such a des-

1654.

pisable Vanitie, and hee hath the more Credit that hee offend not in this way. It striketh mee at this time, as it hath not heretofore that the Scriptures doe oft so speake as though Man's Portion mainly were worthie of consideration, for good or ill, in this Union; this may bee from the Custome of the Countreys in the East, to looke upon a Wife as no more than a Servant: And here wee may observe the change in this respect wrought by our *Saviour*, whose tender Compassion overlooked not the weake and dependant nature of Woman, but raised her up from her low estate; despised not her Humilitie, but accepted her Faith, and opened her Heart to understand his Teachings. No marvell that the Mothers brought their little Children that their Divine Master might blesse them also.

Heare little of any publicke Newes. *Die* sayth manie were greatly scandalized that the *Protector* should goe to a Feast at the *Lord Maior's* on *Ash-Wednesday*, riding in state through the Cittie; Service was forbidden in all the Churches.

May 1, Monday.

Have engaged Mr. *Peter Hingston*, Organist of St. *Marys* Church in *Ipswich*, to come to *Parham* one day in the weeke; the Girles mightily pleafed, and promife to bee diligent Schollers. He is Nephew to Mr. *John Hingston*, the Organift to the *Protector*, who hath had the Organe of *Magdalen Colledge* brought from *Oxford* and put up at *Hampton Court*, where he delighteth in hearing it as hee walketh in the greate Gallerie. Mr. *Hingston* fayth his Highneffe hath alfo a love for Singing, and hath Concerts performed before him, and fo pleafed was he with the Singing of one Mr. *Quin*, that he reftored him to his Student's place in *Chrift-Church*, from which he had beene turned out.

Sentence hath beene executed on Mr. *Gerrard* and one named *Vowel*, taken in the late Confpiracie, likewife the *Portugal* Ambaffador's Brother, their time of probation cut fhort by Man's cruell Judgements, and their Soules hurried unbidden into the Prefence of their *Creator:* when will the End of fuch things bee? when will Man as well as the Angels rejoyce over the Sinner that repenteth?

Letter from my *Daughter*, the little *Heneage* in good Health, and likely to bee off on his Feet before he is much older.

It was reported in *Ipfwich* that the *Protector* was killed, fome faid by a Piftoll Shot.

1654.

June 21, *Wednefday*.

October 3, *Tuefday*.

From the Diary of

1654.
October 4, Wednesday.

The Newes of the Death of the *Protector* proves to have beene a false Report, yet was hee not farre off such an Accident; having a minde to drive his owne Coach drawne by the six Horses lately given to him by the Duke of *Oldenburgh*, hee did provoke them with the Whip, which made them unruly, and his *Highnesse* was flung from off the Coach-box, and his Feet being caught in the Tackling he was dragged some way: the report of the Pistoll occasioned some present to thinke he was Shot; but it was found to bee one which hee did weare concealed, and this hath beene much commented on, as no one did imagine that he stood in so great Feare of his Life as to carrie Fire-armes about his Person.

Dec. 10, Sunday.

Much Sicknesse and Want among our poore Neighbours: not a day passeth but that some one or other sendeth up to the *Hall* for Phisicke or Helpe of some sort. Our stocke of Linsie Woolsie hath beene of good service, also a Cloth called Fustian, made in the north, called *Bolton* Cloth. *Fanny* is now rewarded for her diligence in her Herbe Garden and the Still-roome, and hath given out divers Medicines with her owne Hands, which have proved serviceable, and comforting Cordials and Syrops for the old and weakely, which shee doth oft take to those that are bed-rid, and returneth rich in the Blessings of the Poore and those readie to perish.

In some solicitude for my Daughter *Winchelsea*, who looketh to the encrease of her Familie in another month or thereabout; when writing to her by Mr. *Gage* did call to her Remembrance the 15 Verse of the 2nd. Chapter of St. *Paul's* 1st *Epistle to Timothy*. The *Lord* blesse her and keepe her, the *Lord* blesse her evermore.

From the Diary of

1654-5.

Feb. 17, Saturday.

Y Lord *Newport* came yesternight, and this evening arrived Sir *Henry Slingsby* and one other, who departed after Supper.

Feb. 20, Tuesday.

Letter from my Daughter *Winchelsea*, shee doth write cheerfully, and says shee hath recovered wonderfully well; the Infant thrives, & her little *Heneage* is mightily pleased with his Sister; when shee cries, he runnes up to kisse her, and is disturbed to find it of no availe: may my deare *Daughter's* Nurserie be to her an encreasing Joy, and repaie her for all that shee hath gone through.

Feb. 23, Friday.

How greatly to my comfort and happinesse would it bee if my *Husband* would keepe from meddling in the Affaires of either Partie, and live in such retirement as doth now Sir *Harry Vane*,

Lady Willoughby.

1654-5.

who abideth quietly at *Raby;* alſo another of his former Friends, Colonell *Hutchinſon*, who hath ſtirred not in publicke Matters for ſome time; I have heard ſaie hee did ſoone ſuſpect the Deſigns of *Cromwell*, and was held in ſmall favour by him, this the more that he ſpake with plaineneſſe and Sinceritie when words of Complement would have beene more acceptable, hereby giving offence, as was evident and much noted at the time, in the neglect purpoſely ſhewn to him at the Funerall of Generall *Ireton:* Col. *Hutchinſon,* it is ſayd, doeth great good in his part of the Countrey as a Magiſtrate, and doth give up much of his Time in endevour to improve the People in his Neighbourhood: a Kinſman of Mrs. *Hutchinſon* who had lately viſited *Awthorpe,* and paſſed by this way on his journey homeward, did give us a pleaſing Relation of Mr. *Hutchinſon's* care for the Education and Amuſement of his Children, providing for them Maſters in Muſicke and Painting. Hee hath an ardent love for Painting, and hath become poſſeſſ'd of ſeverall choice Pictures of the late *King's,* ſome of which hee did buy from thoſe who had received them for Wages or Money owing to them, before that the *Protector* had put a ſtop to the Sale.

From the Diary of

1654-5.
March 24, Saturday.

My deare *Husband* came home with a disturbed Countenance. The Government has beene verie busie with Arrests and Examinations; a Friend in *London* writes there is a report much credited that the *King* is in this Countrey: it is pretie well knowne that my Lord *Rochester* is skulking about, and divers Gentlemen are under suspicion: feared to aske any Question: Sir *Henry Slingsby* came at night-fall.

March 27, Tuesday.

My *Daughter* writes that the eldest *Child* is sicke.

March 28, Wednesday.

Another Letter; my little *Grandsonne* worse.

Deare *Mother*,

    Heneage is very ill, and the Physitions thinke that *Babie* is sickening of the Disease. The *Earle* not having had the Small-pox, has yielded to my entreatie that hee would keepe out of the way of Infection as much as possible; but he will not leave the House, and, deare *Mother*, sheweth tender care for mee and the *Children:*

      asking your Prayers, I am
        your dutifull *Daughter*,
          D. *Winchelsea.*

March 30, Friday.

The precious *Child* is removed. Have writt

to my poore bereaved *Daughter;* fcarce, meethinks, can there be a chance for the *Babie's*
Life. My deare *Hufband* much moved by the
Loffe of his fweet *Grandfonne,* and we wept
together at the thought that we fhould fee his
little merrie Face no more.

Madame,
    It is with unfpeakable Griefe that I have
to informe your *Ladyfhipp* of the Deceafe
of my *Sonne,* who departed this Life at 9
o'clocke this Morning. The *Infant* is no
better; but the Feaver is not fo greate as
was the little *Boyes,* and my deare *Wife* doth
continue to hope it will be fpared to comfort
us for our heavy Loffe: I beg your *Ladyfhip*
to excufe more at this time from,
    Madame, your *Ladyfhip's*
  Affectionate and humble Servant,
              Winchelfea.

Letter from the Earle of Winchelfea.

    To-day have received another Letter from
my Lord *Winchelfea;* the little Infant is re-
leafed. My poore *Daughter's* forrow unexpreff-
able, both her precious Babes taken! *Heavenly
Father,* comfort and fupport her under this

April 2, Monday.

1655.

*April 4,
Wednesday.*

afflicting Dispensation of thy *Providence.* My poore Child!

Have beene pleased to see the Sympathie felt by all our Houshold in this season of Trouble; the Women can scarce speake for crying when they aske how my *Daughter* bears the Losse of her sweet *Children: Fanny* & *Elizabeth* greatly distressed, they doe heartily love their *Sister:* this is the first Bereavement they have suffered.

*April 8,
Sunday.*

An unfinished Letter from my poore afflicted *Daughter* sent mee by her *Husband,* who doth adde to it a fewe Lines, hee found it on her Table, shee having beene carried to bed by her Maids, too ill to continue writing: my Heart is pierced through by her Suffering. Have mercie, oh *God,* upon thy afflicted Handmaiden, strengthen her Faith, binde up her broken Heart, and pour the oile of Consolation into her wounded Affection. Shee mourneth as *Rachel* for her *Children,* and will not bee comforted. Unto thy Fatherly Care doe I commit her, in the blessed Assurance that shee will be brought to know thee, the *God of all Consolation.*

Letter of
Ladie
Winchelsea.

Deare *Mother,*

All is now so changed I wonder that I

Lady Willoughby.

Live. My Teares seeme frozen up, and a heavie Weight is at my Heart.

Deare *Mother*, I am a little better; in very miserie I crawled up to the Nurserie, the Cradle and the little Bed, they were there: but my *Children*, my precious ones: I kneeled downe and tried to praie, and so wept. Were my Prayers too wilfull, that *God* heard mee not when I prayed night and day for the Life of my Darlings? Is *my God thy God*, Mother? *thou* prayest and Hee answereth thee; but Hee is far from me, childlesse, comfortlesse.

Writt to my beloved *Daughter*, but could onely feebly expresse what I would faine give utterance to of my tender Sympathie, and intreatie that shee would submit to the Chastening of Him *who doth not willingly afflict*: Exhorted her to seeke for the onely true Peace promised by the *Saviour*, the Peace he left to his Disciples, of Love and perfect Obedience, even to the Death of the Crosse; and did conclude with a few words on Praier, which I humbly hope may be some helpe to her. I cannot suffer for her; but I doe suffer with her, my deare afflicted *Child*.

1655.

April 9, Monday.

From the Diary of

1655.

April 23, Monday.

While yet in much sadnesse my *Husband* perplexed by the Newes that Sir *Henry Slingsby* is arrested, and others, and hath delayed his Journey into *Leicestershire*. He hath information from a Friend that in the examinations of one *Jones*, reported to Secretary *Thurlowe*, the Lord *Willoughby's* name is mentioned, that hee was to bee a Generall and head the rising in *Yorkshire*; severall Gentlemen taken in *Shropshire*. Could no longer conceale my Feares, and urged him with every the most earnest Perswasion to have no more part in these vaine Attempts. How short a time is it since the last Victims were brought to Death. Alas! naught that I can saie availeth, and no measure of Prudence that I can devise, can cover his Rashnesse; not that indeed he acknowledgeth to the truth of my Suspicions, but says Women are alwayes thinking there must be something dangerous if a Man doe but stirre ever so little.

June 2, Saturday.

My *Husband* hath intelligence that Warrants are out against him and my Lord *Newport*, and his Brother Mr. *Seymour*, and other Gentlemen: He will not conceale himselfe, saying there can nothing bee proved against him. Hee hath of purpose hidde from mee some late

Lady Willoughby.

Tranfactions, the fo doing hee did entreat mee to confider no want of belief in my Prudence, feeing there could by no poffibilitie bee one in whom hee could more furely truft, or whofe Counfell hee would more defire, but the Safetie of himfelfe and his Familie and others, did make this the moft prudent courfe. Hee did kindly enter into fome Particulars. An Order hath lately paffed the *Councell,* that all with Eftates above 100 pounds yearely value, who at any time have taken up Armes for the *King,* fhall pay a Tenth of their Propertie to *Government.* Something like, fayd hee, the old affaire of Ship Money: alfo another mode of raifing Money is fet on foote; the whole Countrey is divided; and officers, whom they ftyle *Major Generalls,* appointed over each Divifion, who fine and fend to Prifon whom they pleafe, under pretence of beeing delinquents: this Oppreffion not likely to be borne. In the afternoone he rode toward *Colchefter,* where fome one was to meete him: *Wingfield* had gone on before with a led Horfe.

Wingfield returned, and fayth his *Lord* was gone on to *London,* and did defire I would make myfelfe eafie; more eafie to bee defired than to bee done. Did refraine queftioning

1655.

June 3, Sunday.

1655.

June 6,
Wednesday.

June 14,
Thursday.

Wingfield more closely, possibly he hath beene commanded silence.

Not long have I had to waite for those Tidings which I knew must arrive; So soone as hee reached *London* last *Saturday*, my deare *Life* was arrested and carried straight to the *Tower*, at the same time with my Lord *Newport* and Mr. *Seymour*.

Left without any Directions, have determined to take *Fanny* and *Elizabeth* and follow him to *London*: Interest must be made with all our Friends: now is it well for us that my Lord *Lisle* declined going on the Embassage to *Sweden*, and is in *London* at this time. The Lord *Say* too will give us helpe.

With *Fanny's* assistance chose some Lodgings in *Leadenhall Street*, leaving her *Sister* at my Lord *Winchelsea's*; would faine have left *Fanny* also, but shee could by no persuasion bee prevailed upon, and a deare Comfort shee is to mee. The young Man *Lydgate* seemes likely to suite; hee is active, and though quiet is not easily daunted, and hath good stocke of common sense: When his Brother was killed in the North, his Mother tooke to her Bed, and soone after died, bidding her Sonne with her last breath come up to the *Hall* and saie that

Lady Willoughby.

Peggy Lydgate did pray mee to take into my Service the Sonne whose Life I had saved; and a faithfull Ladde hee hath beene and seemeth like to bee.

Refused Admittance to the *Tower*, strict orders are given that no Friends of the Prisoners bee admitted: Sent *Lydgate* back to the *Tower*, carrying with him Linnen, Wine, and other matters for the dear Prisoner; when hee returned sayd my *Lord* was greatly chafed at this misadventure, yet hath hee no Misgivings of his Safetie as to his Life; for how long a time he may bee shut up in Prison, it liketh him not to thinke. Divers other Gentlemen are in the *Tower*, Sir *Frederick Cornwallis*, the Lord *Maynard*, Sir *Geoffrey Palmer*, and others: Could scarce sleepe at night, disturbed by present Feares and past Remembrances.

Tooke a Coach and drove to *Charter House Square*: My Lord *Grey* not at home; then to *Northumberland House*; got sight of Lord *Lisle* with some difficulty. Hee doth assure mee that hee beleeveth the Gentlemen now in the *Tower* are put there more to keepe them from doing Mischief than with any intent to bring them to a Triall. *His Highnesse*, then, sayd I, scrupleth not at Starre Chamber Practice,

1655.

June 15, Friday.

June 16, Saturday.

1655.

and innocent Men are shut up in Prison at his pleasure without proofe of being guiltie, or opportunitie given to shew their innocence. He made replie with some Harshnesse of manner, *My Lord* Willoughby *may bee innocent in your Ladyship's Eyes, but his treasonable Designes are so well knowne that his best Friends may bee glad of what your Ladyship is pleased to call Starre Chamber Practise.* He then added more mildly, that hee hoped wee would bee patient, and promised he would use his utmost Indeavour to procure leave for mee to see my *Husband*. Mr. *Algernon Sydney* here entered the Roome, and his Brother introduced him to mee, and I rose about to take my leave; when Mr. *Sydney* begged to detaine me for a short time: Hee then repeated what his Brother had before said, and proceeded to say that he had that esteeme for my Lord *Willoughby* that hee did desire he should not misjudge him in the matter of the late *King's* Triall and Death. Hee was present on the first day of the Triall, but did see then a sterne Resolve in the Countenance of some which did alarm him as also Coll. *Hutchinson*, and forthwith he departed the House, seeing it was too strong a Current for him to checke, and remained at *Penshurst*. All *Eng-*

lishmen hee conceived were called upon to refist the tyrannous and unconstitutional Government of the late *King*, but to the Necessitie of the last murderous Act, he would never subscribe: What Measure might have beene adopted it were uselesse now to enquire; he did beleeve those who were at the Head of the State were men of honest Views and Intentions in the beginning; but there had beene a graduall Change in some, and a dangerous Ambition stirring in one Minde, whereof it was not expedient to speake openly; the End would shortly come. No great Evill can be remedied without Evill ensuing in the processe; honest Men must hold fast to the Good to be obtained, even though they may bee drawne into the Whirlepoole of man's worst Passion, and suffer the Shame of man's worst deeds, an honest Man must abide by the Truth; ay, and die for the Truth. He did appear to forget to whom he spake, his sterne voice softened as he begged mee not to be alarmed; my *Husband's* Life he knew to bee in no jeopardie. I tooke my leave in some Agitation: I had looked at these Things from a distance, now I beheld one of the Actors in the struggle, and my feeble Spirit quailed at

1655.

the Sight: fervently thanked *God* that the awful Triall of giving up Life for the Truth had not beene apportioned to mee, or to thofe neare and deare unto mee.

June 17, Sunday.

My Lord *Lifle* called; he had beene to *Whitehall*, but could not get an Audience with the *Protector*, but hath engaged Mr. *Thurlow* in our Behalf, who hath promifed his Influence.

June 18, Monday.

Mr. *Evelyn* came; he doth propofe to carrie backe with him my Daughter *Fanny* to *Sayes Court*, and alfo expreffes an earneft defire that fhee may accompanie him to the *Tunbridge Wells*: gave my Confent gladly, beleeving that the Waters of that place would be of Service to her Health, not that fhee ftands fo much in need of Improvement in that refpect as fhee once did.

My *Sifter* came and tooke mee to fuppe with her.

June 20, Wednefday.

Yefterday beeing *Lord's Day*, and having heard mention that at the Church of St. *Gregorie* was ftill ufed the Church Forme of Service, the Liturgie, &c. and beeing defirous to heare the fame, went there. Heard Dr. *Wild* preach. Church well attended. Returned home by the *Strand*; my *Daughter* but poorely; if through mercie fhee keepe up through this Month I shall be more at ease concerning her.

Our Friends, after using every means, could onely obtaine Permission that I should see my *Husband* during the space of one houre, and this in the presence of two of the Soldiers on guard: my Lord *Lisle* did with much kindnesse, advise mee to appeare at ease, and talke of indifferent Matters, and seeme to be under no concerne that my *Lord* was there for a few dayes or weekes.

Went to the *Tower;* hard work to maintaine a cheerefull Countenance, say rather to keep up a cheerefull Heart, not much reall gaine if there is the one and not the other.

Found *Fanny* returned from her Visite: shee doth looke sweetly, and nothing loth to tell of all shee hath seene and heard. Mrs. *Evelyn* hath showne her most kind and loving Condescention, and is a Gentlewoman of rare Accomplishment and amicable Disposition, and doeth all things that shee doth undertake excellently well. Mr. *Evelyn* is busied with his Alterations and Improvements at *Sayes Court*. The Gardens, which he laid out two yeares since, are filled with thriving Plants, divers sortes of Roses and other rare and beautious

1655.

Flowers, more particularly such as are of pleasant Perfume and Fragrancy, for which he hath peculiar liking. Also he cultivates such Herbes as will supplie Honie for his Bees, which he doth keepe in a transparent Hive given to him by Dr. *Wilkins*, of *Oxforde*. *Fanny* omitted no Partikilar, it is so constructed, one upon another, that the Honie can be taken without the crueltie of destroying the Bees: He made her a Drawing of the Plan, and writt full and plaine directions for the Management of Bees. Also did he, with condescention and courtesie provide for her Entertainment within doors, shewing her the arte of graving on Copper Plates, and gave her a Print done by himselfe of his dear *Wotton*, likewise his Picture engrav'd by a Sculptor at *Paris*, much like: methought shee did slightly blush when shee spoke of a Mr. *Brereton*, a young Gentleman held in greate esteeme by Mr. *Evelyn*: So much to bee told of *Sayes Court*, description of *Tunbridge Wells* left for another time.

Sept. 15, Saturday.

Mett Mr. *Evelyn* in the *Park* to day, tooke occasion to inquire somewhat particularly of his friend Mr. *Brereton*, he did willingly enter on the subject. He is the Sonne of my Lord *Brereton* and hath lately come to *England*,

Lady Willoughby.

having beene at *Breda* for his Education fome yeares, and is a very accomplifhed Gentleman; his Father's Eftates are much involved through the late Troubles, in affifting the *King*.

 Met at Dinner, Mr. *Pepys*, Mr. *Evelyn*, and the Lord *Baltimore*, who feemeth a Gentleman of moft rare Excellence and Ability. Hee difcourfed very agreeably, and gave the Companie a long and full Hiftorie of the founding of *Maryland*. He was now in *London* to petition the *Protector* to iffue an order to the Governour of *Virginia* that there fhould be no Interference on his part with the Government of *Maryland*, that Countrey having flourifht beyond all others under the Laws and Regulations he had inftituted. Hee had mett with a courteous reception at *Whitehall*.

 Went to the *Tower* as ufuall, the Day bitter cold : in the Evening fupped with my Daughter *Winchelfea*, Mr. *Brereton* there.

 This day all Minifters of the Church of *England* forbidden Preaching and Teaching. Thus while wee make collection of Money to affift the Perfecuted in forreine Countreys; the fpirrit of Perfecution burnes hotely in our owne.

 Yefterday Sir *Robert Stone* tooke us to fee

1655.

Sept. 18,
Tuefday.

Nov. 9,
Friday.

Nov. 27,
Tuefday.

Dec. 13,
Thurfday.

Whitehall, hee gained Admittance through some small Acquaintance he had with Sir *Oliver Flemming* Master of the Ceremonies: as wee passed through a Roome called the *Greene Chamber* wee were told it was there the late *King* was permitted to retire with the *Bishop*; remaining there some time private in order to the receiving the *Sacrament* about an houre or so before his Execution: As wee did enter the Gallerie wee saw divers Gentlemen passing out by another Doore, and learned that a Conference had then ended: wee stayed to looke at the Pictures, some still remaining, also some fine Tapestries in another Apartment which wee did see afterward, and so it was that a Doore at the other side of the Gallerie was throwne open; Sir *Oliver Flemming* and others stood in attendance, and presently his *Highnesse* appeared engaged in Discourse with a man strangely apparelled and of remarkable Countenance, and wearing a long Beard; wee kept as much out of sight as wee could and were in part concealed by a doore way: The *Protector* advanced but a few Steppes along the Gallerie, as it seemed, to conclude that which hee was saying, then making a Salutation to him to whom he spake, hee retired whence he came.

Lady Willoughby.

Meeting Sir *Oliver* ere wee left the Palace, hee informed us that the Stranger in the forreine Garbe whom wee had juft feene, was the Jewifh Rabbi *Menaffeh Ben Ifrael*, fent over from *Holland* by the *Jewes* who defire Permiffion to eftablifh fome of their Nation in this Countrey; a Councell was held this morning to confider of their Propofitions, the *Protector* looketh favorably on their Petition.

Had an opportunitie this day of gaining fome further Information on the fubject of the *Jewes*, it affected mee not a little in thinking on our returne home from *Whitehall*, that wee had looked upon one of that defpifed People the Rejectors of the *Meffiah* and the Imprecators of the Curfe upon themfelves and upon their Children: yet a People highly favored by the *Moft High*.

It did happen that as I was fpeaking of the circumftance of our feeing the *Rabbi*, one prefent expreffed his Hope that the *Jewes* would bee admitted into *England*. Dr. *Wilkins*, (of *Oxford*,) anfwered him, Did he know that they were for having St. *Paul's* for their Synagogue, and the *Bodleian Librarie* at *Oxford* to bee given into their keeping. He had beene told they had offered the *Protector* 500,000 Pounds

1655.

Dec. 14, Friday.

if these two Points were yeilded, to which hee was willing enough to agree, but others would not. There was a Reason whispered about that the *Jewes* were for making out the *Protector* to bee the expected *Messiah;* and it was knowne to not a few that some *Jewes* had beene searching through the Librarie at *Cambridge* for Bookes relating to Prophesies, and afterwarde did goe downe to *Huntingdon* where *Cromwell* was borne, to get knowledge of his Familie and Ancestors; but this was noised abroad, and it was thought prudent to dismisse them the Countrey: these *Jewes* were from the *Levant*, but it is not unlikely that this hath beene pleasing to the *Protector*, and made him well disposed to favor the Deputation from *Holland*. I did listen with much attention to all that was sayd, and have here put it downe, as it seemeth to mee something wonderfull, that the *Jewes* should hold this opinion of *Cromwell*, and likewise it is curious to see the hidden motive to Men's Actions.

Dec. 25, Tuesday.

No Churches open: We heard there was private Service in some Families; I went to a Chappell near by.

Word early this morning from my Lord *Winchelsea* that my *Daughter* was ailing.

Went to the *Tower*, tooke leave of my *Husband*; my deare Life ill at eafe, affected with Cold and fome Feaver, no doubt caufed by his damp and miferable Lodging, and want of all Comforts: The wretch *Baxter* taketh a Pleafure in treating his Prifoners defpitefully.

Found *Die* in prettie good Heart, and difpofed to fleepe.

This afternoone my deare *Daughter* fafely brought to bed; returned heartfelt Thankes to *Almightie God* for this great Mercie: the *Infant* weakely, but with Care and good Nurfing likely enough to live.

A fmile of peacefull Happineffe on my beloved *Child's* Face as fhee lay with the *Babie* on her Arme, fuch as I have not feene there for long. May fhee be reftored to Health, and the little one be fpared to be a prefent Joy and a Crowne of rejoycing to her latter dayes. Her *Sifters* fcarce take their eyes off, or doe anything but rocke the Cradle and watch *Nurfe*. Sent to the *Tower* to gladden the Heart of the poore Prifoner by the good tidings.

1655.

Dec. 29, Saturday.

1655-6.

Feb. 11, Monday.

1655-6.

WEnt to the *Tower*, thence to call at Mr. *Evelyn's* Lodgings by *Covent Garden*, where I did incounter the unhappie Widow of the Lord *Capel*, her Daughter newly maried, Ladie *Beauchamp* was alſo preſent; a Gentlewoman of gracefull Cariage, and ſeemingly of ſweet ingenuous Temper. Mention beeing made of Dr. *Peter Heylyn*, Mr. *Evelyn* related ſome anecdotes of divers Frights and Diſaſters which befell him in the late troublous Times; and the great loſſe he had in his Bookes, which were all taken from him, and manie of them ſold by the Soldiers for a flagon of Ale. Hee, on one occaſion, when he left his Hiding-place in the diſguiſe of a poore wayfaring Man, beeing mett by ſome Soldiers, one of them

Lady Willoughby.

laying hold of his Hand, felt a Ring under his Glove, and so did conclude him a runnaway *Cavalier;* but by a good Chance for him they were disturbed in the Robberie of this good man, and missed finding some Peeces of Gold he had hidde in his High Shooes. Of late hee hath retired to a Farme (beeing silenced preaching,) in *Oxfordshire.* Mrs. *Evelyn* read some Verses of his, writt when hee was a Suitor to the Ladie he did afterwarde marie, and presented to her with a rich gilded *Bible,* and I admiring them, Mrs. *Evelyn* did lend them to mee, that if I so pleased I might copie them, and then returne them to her. This I have done.

These by Dr. *Peter Heylin,* given with a *Bible.*

Could this outside beholden bee
To cost and cunning equally;
Or were it such as might suffice
The luxurie of curious Eyes;
Yet would I have my Deerest looke
Not on the Cover, but the Booke.

If thou art merie, here are Aires;
If melancholie, here are Prayers:

If studious, here are those things writ
 Which may deserve thy ablest Wit;
If hungry, here is Food Divine;
 If thirsty, Nectar, heavenly Wine.

Read then, but first thyselfe prepare
 To read with Zeale, and marke with Care;
And when thou read'st what here is writt
 Let thy best Practice second it;
So twice each Precept read shall bee,
 First in the Booke and next in Thee.

Much reading may thy Spirits wrong:
 Refresh them, therefore, with a Song:
And that thy Musicke praise may merite,
 Sing David's Psalms with David's Spirit;
That as thy Voice doth pierce Men's Ears,
 So shall thy Prayers and Vows the Spheres.

Thus read, thus sing, and then to thee
 The very Earth a Heaven shall bee:
If thus thou readest, thou shalt find
 A private Heaven within thy Minde:
And singing thus before thou die,
 Thou sing'st thy part to those on High.

St. *Valentine's* Day. Feb. 14, *Thursday.*

At an early Houre this morning a small Packet was left by a serving Man wearing a

Lady Willoughby.

Liverie not knowne to *Lydgate*, who tooke it from him. It was addreſſed to Miſtreſs *Frances Willoughby ; Fanny* received it with an abaſhed Countenance as her eye caught the writing of the Superſcription, which Character did not ſeeme altogether ſtrange to her. Within the outmoſt paper was a Letter tied with ſilke. She quickly handed it to mee to open, but I would not ſo diſhonour St. *Valentine*, and left her to penetrate the Myſterie. The Cuſtome is in my minde a harmleſſe one. Innocent in beeing generall, and in its poeticall and fancifull guiſe partaking ſomewhat of the Ancient chivalrous Character: No doubt the *Knight* in this little piece of Gallantrie, is a certaine Gentleman whoſe Attention will not be diſpleaſing to the faire young Maiden ; who can ſay that ſhee will not ſometime looke backe upon this very Day with a mournefull Pleaſure, but I will checke my penne, nor diſturb even in Imagination what is perhaps the firſt whiſper of Love to her young Heart: it may not bee ſo, but I know not a more bleſſed Reliefe to my concerne for this deare *Child*, than that no mariage Contract ſhould be made for *her*, unſanctified by a ſweet and holie Affection. Cuſtome hath led us wrong in this

1655-6.

matter, in the difpofal of one dearely loved *Daughter*, not fo fhall it againe: I have heard fay that an overture of mariage was made by my Lord *Leicefter*, who did afke my hand for his Sonne, Lord *Lifle*, which was refpectfullie declined by my honoured *Father*: I was of tender Yeares; and my *Mother* approved not of engagements entered into for Parties in their Childhood.

Feb. 22, Friday.

Yefternight the houfe of the *Swedifh* Ambaffador was curioufly lighted up, painted tranfparent Papers were put into the Frames of the Windowes, the glaffe Panes beeing taken away, and Candles were placed behind the Paintings. In the Balcones on each fide of the Houfe were Trumpets, 7 or 8 founded together: The occafion of all this to celebrate the Birth of the *Swedifh* Prince.

March 4, Tuefday.

As I was prepared to fet forth to the *Tower*, Word was brought me that my Daughter *Winchelfea* was greatly alarmed about her *Babie*, which had beene fuddenly feized with Convulfions in the night; though partly recovered, fhee did very earneftly intreat mee to come to her; after my Returne from the *Tower*, I came hither and found the *Child* better.

Lady Willoughby.

To day the *Child* doth appeare well, save some slight Indisposition occasioned seemingly by the disagreement of its Food, my *Daughter* cheery, but no wonder shee is soone alarmed. *1655-6. March 5, Wednesday.*

The poore *Babie* seized with another Fitte and scarce could live through it; the *Mother* holdeth it in her Armes and will suffer none other to take it. *March 7, Friday.*

Againe hath the *Lord* visited us with Affliction, my little *Grandchild* breathed its last on *Sunday* night; my *Daughter's* state beeing but weakely, and shee worne out with Nursing and Anxietie of Heart, now lyeth dangerously ill. *March 11, Tuesday.*

The Feavor increasing and her Senses wander, another *Physition* called in. *March 14, Friday.*

Still is there Hope as one of the Doctors sayd to mee, there is no telling what the Young will struggle through, but her Health and Spirits have beene terribly shaken; my *Sister* hath taken away *Fanny* and *Elizabeth*, to bee out of the way of Infection; my *Husband* hath many Feares for me, I am wonderfully preserved from Apprehension, but to satisfie him take all the Precaution in my power, and doe weare Bags of Camphire sewed into my Dresse, and smell oft at a small grated Box *March 15, Saturday.*

1655-6.

March
Sunday.

one of the *Physitions* did give me, filled with some strong Aromatique which some do consider a sure Preservative.

The Doctors thinke some Symptomes more favourable: may the *Lord* blesse their Endeavours to restore this deare *Child*.

Mr. *Evelyn*, who hath great Ingenuity, sent mee a night Lampe, made of a large lumpe of Wax, which lighted and set in a silver Bason, giveth out a very small Flame and lasteth manie Nights.

March 19,
Wednesday.

Againe worse; my Lord *Winchelsea* is for having more Advice, but hath yeelded to our opinion, that having already 5 *Physitions*, and these of most Eminence, nothing would be gained, but the rather Inconvenience by more.

March 20,
Thursday.

To-day all Hope is given up, knew not how to find Wordes to tell the sad Newes to my poore *Husband;* now indeed is the bitternesse of our Separation fully experienced, his *Daughter* dying, and he shut up in Prison.

March 22,
Saturday.

At 5 o'Clocke yesterday Morning, my beloved Daughter *Diana fell asleepe* in the 21st yeare of her Age, a short Life in which shee had past through a deepe Baptisme; *God's* will be done.

March 26,
Wednesday.

Looked for the last time on the deare

Lady Willoughby.

Remaines; much broken in fpirit and very forrowfull, yet I mourned not as one without hope, and was enabled to attaine unto a good degree of Compofure ere I turned away from the fweete placid Countenance. Tooke from between the leaves of my *Bible* a few withered Flowers, and gently laid them on her Breaft: kiffed the peaceful Face of my beloved *Child*, and left the Chamber. As I foftly clofed the Doore and felt that never more——

Take up the Penne, but what can I fay? *Lord, I beleeve, helpe thou mine unbeleefe. Father, not my Will, but Thine be done.*

As the Hart panteth after the water-brooks, fo panteth my Soule after Thee, O God. Beene favoured to approach to fome Foretafte of this Heavenly State, as I was led this morning in the Solitude of my Clofet into deep Meditation on the Holineffe and Perfection of the *Divine Being*. My foule feemed readie to crie out, Do with me as thou wilt, O *God*, to lead mee unto thyfelfe: yet fo foone as the Prayer was uttered, my poor fearfull Nature trembled; *The Spirit is willing, but the Flefh is weake.* Gracious words from *Him* who was tried as wee are, yet without Sinne.

My *Daughter* and pretty *Grandchildren* all

1656.

March 28, *Friday.*

March 30, *Sunday.*

1656.

taken; I can truly fay, that for my precious *Child*'s fake I can rejoyce that fhee is removed from this Life of Sorrow; bereaved of her fweet *Children*, and of the laft juft as fhee had tafted once more of a Mother's joy, her over-grieved Heart could no more fuftaine this frefh Griefe, and fhee has followed them no more to be feparated.

Mournefull is it to the more advanced in Yeares, to fee the Young taken, the *Infant* of a few dayes and the youthfull *Mother*, whileft the aged Pilgrim is left to defcend with feeble Step into *The Valley of the Shadow of Death*. The *Lord's* will be done. May I more and more ftrive to bee prepared to give an Account of my Stewardfhip, whenfoever it may be his will to fummon me hence.

It hath beene a time of deepe and tender Exercife of Spirit as I kept watch by the Sicke bed; gracioufly vifited by fweet Tokens of the *Divine Prefence*, and enabled to refigne this precious Object of my Love and tender Solicitude, comforted to know that fhee had found *Chrift* to be indeed *the Way, the Truth, and the Life*. There were but few Seafons of Confcioufneffe and they fhort, as a Stupor fucceeded to the Delirium; once toward the

Lady Willoughby.

1656.

laſt ſhee opened her eyes, and fixed them upon mee with a pitifull looke, and her Lippes moved, but there was no articulate Sound, poore Thing! the Change to her is doubtleſſe a happie one, but to mee a heavie and grievous Loſſe, ſhee was ever a dearely loved *Child*, and of late my Heart had beene drawne to her in neare Sympathie in her many Trialls. Her *Siſters* doe take this Sorrow much to Heart, and weepe for her and the little Babe.

April 17, *Thurſday.*

The Impriſonnement of my deare *Huſband* becometh greatly weariſome to him. He doth now often wiſh that hee had not returned to *England*, but had ſtayed to manage his Affaires in *Antigua*, ſaying to-day when the time drew neare for mee to take my Leave, that hee would more willingly bee ſeparated from us by the wide Sea, than the thicke Walls of the *Tower*, prevented the free uſe of his Limbs, and denied the freſh Aire, and expoſed to the Inſolence of the *Governour*. Beholding him thus chafed, propoſed to goe myſelfe to the *Protector*, and petition for his Releaſe, but this angered him mightily. Doe ſuppoſe it is more difficult to Man's nature to be patient than it is to us: Accuſtomed to reſiſt and overcome Difficultie and Danger, it is a ſurpriſe

1656.

to them when it doth happen otherwife; and whatfoever they may fuffer, if like occafion offer againe, feldome are they deterred from the fame conduct. At this time, beleeve my *Lord* would, if hee were given his Libertie, plunge into the firft Scheme that was contrived as hopefull of Succeffe, as though they had never failed in Attempts which have hitherto ended onely in Death or Captivitie: He did urge upon mee to leave this wearie Citie; *The fweet Aire of Parham would better thy Health, deare Wife:* this he fayd as he did tenderly remarke on my pale and worne Lookes, and my Haire turning graie. *And yet it will goe hard to part with fuch a loving Caretaker, the onely deare Comfort I have.* Would not confent to leave *London;* on the contrarie, would defire to ftay with him altogether in the *Tower*, but this hee will never heare mee fpeake of. Reached my Lodging well nigh fpent.

April 21, Monday.

Through the Kindneffe and Perfeverance of our Friends, my *Hufband* hath the Libertie of the *Tower* allowed him: They have entered into Securitie for him, and it is to be hoped his Health will bee amended now that hee hath fome fpace to take Exercife, and can breathe the open Aire.

Lady Willoughby.

1656.
May 2,
Friday.

Spent thefe few Dayes paſt in the houſe, beeing under the neceſſitie of taking ſome reſt. Looked over ſome Papers of my poore *Daughter* which my Lord *Wincheſſea* hath forwarded to mee, they did conſiſt chiefly of Letters, and of theſe not manie: one Paper carefully folded contained ſome Verſes of *Fanny's*, which I have copied before giving them backe to her keeping.

On hearing of the Deceaſe of my
deare *Siſter's Babie*, and given
to her by mee.

Through the white covering of its Bed
The Snow-drop lifteth up its Head,
Though fraile it looke, it enters Life
Bravely to beare the winterie ſtrife;
While the more ſweet and tender Flower,
Tranſplanted from its native Bower,
And balmy Aire, and ſunnie Skies,
Droops its faire Forme, and fades and dyes.
So this ſweete Babie *bloomed awhile,*
And ſmiled to meete its Mother's *ſmile,*
Then for its home in Heaven did pine,
And Death unlooſed life's ſilver Line;

From the Diary of

1656.

> On joyfull wings the Spirit fled,
> Her name recorded with the Dead.
> Frances Willoughby.

At Parham,
April 10, 1654.

On the night when my deare *Daughter* fell ill of that fatall Sicknesse, as wee tooke off her Cloathes, I found a small Packet or case of white Satin worne concealed by her Neck kerchefe, I put it carefully aside at the time, and opening it some fewe dayes after her Decease, did find within the laste fold a silken Locke of pale browne Haire, on the Satin was worked in Gold Thread the letter *H*, and the date of the yeare, 1654: Her darling *Heneage*, the first borne and the first laid in the Grave, soone to bee followed by his little *Sister;* not long, and another *Infant* rested its head on its *Mother's* bosome, this was taken, and now the *Mother's* Triall was over, and shee too was laid beside them.

May 12,
Monday.

Sonnet by my Daughter Fanny.

> This small but costlie Casket, rich inlayed
> With Gems and Ivorie, with Carvings fine

Lady Willoughby.

1656.

> *Of Sandel-wood, its Ebonne ſides to line,*
>   *Whence a ſweet Odour doth the whole pervade;*
> *So ſweet is it, that all things therein laid*
>   *When drawne at times from forth their ſcented*
>   *Shrine*
>   *Do ever beare with them this breathing Signe*
>   *That they have dwelt within its perfumed*
>   *ſhade.*
> *So when the pious and all lowly Heart*
>   *A treſure Houſe is kept wherein doth dwell*
>   *The love of God with moſt deare Conſtancie,*
> *To every word and deed it doth impart*
>   *A Vertue and a gracious Fragrancie*
>   *Which doth to all its hidden worſhip tell.*

Theſe Verſes are to my thinking pretily written, this perhaps not ſurpriſing as we are readie to make much account of what our *Children* do, but yet more is it pleaſing to me to ſee her Fancy thus diſporte itſelfe, drawing good from the little Accidents of Life: when I did expreſſe to her this Satisfaction, ſhee replied that herein ſhee had no Merit, ſhee had been favoured one day, as indeed not ſeldome is our priviledge to enjoy the edifying Diſcourſe of a pious and deare Friend, who did at that time as at many others very feelingly enlarge

1656.

on the indwelling of the *Holy Spirit* and its worke of Regeneration and Sanctification wrought in the Heart, the while hee spake, her eye rested on the little Indian perfume Box, given to her by our young friend Mr. *Brereton*, which stood neare her on the Table; and as shee pondered in silence on the Wordes shee had heard, her Thoughts did thus dresse themselves. Shee hath a great liking for the Sonnet and can repeat by heart many of the most perfect writt in our language, also this taste hath beene encreased by her studie of the *Italian*; with some difficulty I did gain her Permission to show the Poem to him whom I may call the Sower of the good Seed, who doth hold her in his affectionate regard, beleeving that he would receive some Satisfaction in the perusal. Of this Shepheard of the Lord's fold it may bee sayd of him in the exercise of his Ministry, that, in the Wordes of the Psalmist, *He feedeth them according to the integritie of his Heart.*

Sept. 14.

Sir *Henry Vane* is sent Prisoner to *Carrisbrooke Castle*; whence this Severitie of the *Protector* to one who hath used to stand high in his Esteeme and hath done him service is not well knowne: some mention is there of a Booke he hath written.

Lady Willoughby.

1656.
October 2,
Thursday.

Went with Mr. *Evelyn* and his *Wife* downe to *Tunbridge*, and remained there two dayes: there is much building of Houses for the Lodging of Strangers, and for Shops. I have heard say that when the *Queen* resorted thither for the improvement of her Health after the birth of the *Prince*, she was Lodged in Tents sett upp for her on the Down; as the Wells became more frequented, the people set up Standings under the row of Trees in the road to the Well, where they sold their Goods to the Companye who passed bye. We lodged at a pretie Cottage close by the Well: one morning as wee walked under some fine Trees, whose Leaves were beginning to fade, Mr. *Evelyn*, who hath wonderful knowledge of moste things but especiallye of Trees, did point out to mee the new Budde at the foot of the Leafe Stalke, which by its groweth takes up the sappe, and thus the old Leafe doth lose its nourishment and fades and drops off; so that instead of pitying the Trees when they are losing their Leaves, wee should see it only as the preparation for Spring, and a fresher Verdure. Neverthelesse Autumn hath a pleasing sadnesse in its lesson of Change and Death.

At Table one present gave us this Anecdote of

1656.

Sir *Henry Wotton:* Hee being in a Popish Chappel, a Priest that knew him sent a Paper to him with this Query, *Where was your Religion before Luther?* under which he writt these words, *Where yours is not, in the written Word of God.*

October 6, Monday.

Mrs. *Evelyn* tooke us with her to *Pall-Mall.* Chocolate was handed to the Companie in Cups of fine Porcelain, and rare sweetmeats and *Italian* Bisketts: The Lady *Ranelagh* was there on a visite, she mett me courteously, and was pleased to say that her Brother Mr. *Robert Boyle* would regret not seeing mee.

October 7, Tuesday.

The Petition for leave to go to *Surinam* of no availe.

October 27, Monday.

Have remained in the *Tower* since this day senight to attend on my dearest *Life,* who hath beene grievously ill, he is now better and hath walked out twice or thrice.

October 28, Tuesday.

As we were at Dinner to day my *Lord* sayd he beleaved wee were in the same Roome wherein Sir *John Eliot* was imprisoned for so long and died, I asked *who was hee?* He answered that hee was one of the first to suffer when differences began betweene the late *King* and his *Parliament,* one of several Members that were sent to the *Tower,* to bee out of his (the *Kings*) way; He was of a right noble Spirit, and rather than accept the Conditions offered which hee deemed diſhonourable, remained in Priſon, to die a lingering Death from Diſeaſe brought on by his long Captivitie. *I was a Youth*, ſaid my Huſband, *at that time, nigh* 30 *yers ſince, he was much talked about, and I am beholden to him for the firſt ſtirrings in my Heart of a hatred of Tyrannie, ill enough he would thinke I have followed his Example.* Mr. Hampden *knew him well and did honour and eſteeme him beyond any other Man, and after his Death was a Father to his Sonnes: In Countenance he was thought by ſome to bee like the* King; *his Haire and Beard he wore in like faſhion.*

So ill to day feare I can conceale it no longer, as Captain *Butler*, who dined with us, queſtioned mee, and ſo fixed my *Huſband's* attention more on my Lookes, who had at divers times obſerved the Paleneſſe of my Countenance, and that I could with difficultie keepe any Warmth in mee.

Became ſo ill I was like to give up. Some gold peices given to Serjeant *Dendy* had their effect, and the uſe of an inner Roome was permitted us; and, with his wifes helpe, a

1656.

Nov. 28, Friday.

Dec. 4, Thurſday.

1656.

Bed, ſo called, was made up therein; a darke miſerable place, but I was thankefull for the Privacie, and this Woman, who was kindly diſpoſed and ſorry for my Condition, did ſuch little Services ſhee could without danger of obſervation: My *Huſband* hath profitted by his owne Illneſſe, in ſome particulars, to my advantage; eſpecially was hee very alive to the Diſtreſſe occaſioned by Thirſt, and failed not to bring a Cup of Water every time he came to my Bedſide.

Dec. 6, Saturday.

To-day Capt. *Butler* did come to ſee my *Huſband*, and did uſe manie Arguments to perſwade mee to come out from the *Tower;* but I am the more bent upon ſtaying with my *Huſband* now that I know better than I did once what this Impriſonment is; and if to me, who have beene here but a few Weekes, it is ſo miſerable, what muſt it bee to him who hath beene ſhut up theſe 18 Months? Capt. *Butler* did then take a lead Penne and a peece of writing Paper, and wrote. I retired to reſt, and on my returne, my *Lord* ſhewed mee a Letter, and did requeſt me to make a Copie thereof.

Lady Willoughby.

1656. This copy slightly differs from that preserved in Thurlow's State Papers. Ed.

To the *Lord Protector.*

May it pleafe your *Highneſſe,*
   The laſt *Thurſday* I was invited to Dinner with my Lord *Willoughby,* whoſe Ladie is deſperately ſicke; ſhee will not be perſuaded to remove from her *Huſband,* which makes mee moſt humbly requeſt your *Highneſſe,* if his Offence be not great, to grant him the libertie to remove to Sir *Robert Stone's* Houſe in *Tuttle Street.* Thus much I know, that hee is much in Debt, & would willingly goe ſettle either in *Antigo* or *Surinam.* As for his Ladie, ſhee was a great friend to the cauſe of Libertie and true Religion, and it is poſſible things may bee miſinterpreted to your *Highneſſe* concerning her *Huſband.* In this Clemencie of your *Highneſſe* will appear the conqueſt of your Paſſion, which after all my ſadneſſe ſhall oblige mee to remaine
            Your *Highneſſe's*
               moſt humble Servant,
                  though moſt unworthie,
                     Gregorie Butler.
Dec. 6, 1656.

From the Diary of

1656.
Dec. 16,
Tue*s*day.

We heard nothing from Mr. *Butler* till this Day, when hee came he had received a *s*hort Replie from Mr. Secretary *Thurlowe* to this purpo*s*e, that His *Highne*ſſ*e* had knowne the Lord *Willoughby* many Yeares, and that it was through no Mi*s*repre*s*entation that the *s*aid *Lord* found him*s*elfe in his pre*s*ent Situation: the Inconveniencie thereof it re*s*ted not with him to amend. We had encouraged no great Expectation, *s*o were not di*s*appointed, neverthele*ſſ*e, a *s*mall do*s*e of Patience was *s*erviceable.

Dec. 29,
Monday.

Heare with concerne that Doctor *Jeremy Taylor* is *s*ent to the *Tower;* this on *s*o *s*mall an Offence as a Picture beeing *s*et in his Prayer Booke. Letter from *Fanny* to *s*ay my Pre*s*ence is greatly wanted, her *Si*ſ*ter* no better, *s*o have fixed, beleaving it my Duty, to leave this place, which I can do the more ea*s*ily, as my deare *Life* is well recovered.

1657.

May 16,
Saturday.

IT hath beene expected by fome that the *Protector* would have himfelfe crowned *King*, but it having beene propofed in the *Houfe* that a Petition fhould be drawne up, to the effect that they did advife him to take upon himfelfe the Title of *King*, as more confonant to the good of the State and a fettled Government, manie were againft it, and of thefe his oldeft Friends; there not beeing the Unanimitie and Support from thefe hee had looked for, he hath declined the Honour that fome would put upon him; fome, no Friends to him, have had their Hopes raifed by the Attempt; once the tide fet in for *Royaltie*, they thinke the Heart of the People would foone return to its true Allegiance, and the

1657.

Restoration of the rightfull *King* bee the sooner brought about; and if Adversitie hath had its proper use, the *Sonne* might be expected not unreasonably to bee a better *King* than his *Father*, whom men have pitied so much for his Death that his ill Government is well nigh forgotten, and some who were the first to take up Armes in the cause of the People, thinke themselves not much better off.

July 3, Friday.

A great stirre made in *London* last Friday at the Ceremonie of the Inauguration, which was performed with the State and Pompe of the Crowning of a *King*. A rich Cloath of State was set up in *Westminster Hall*, and underneath it a Chair of State up two Steppes covered with Carpets. The *Protector* first passed some Bills in *Parliament*, and then hee went into *Westminster Hall*, attended by Gentlemen and Heraulds and Officers; The Earle of *Warwicke* carrying the Sword before him; The *Speaker* presented to him a Robe of Purple Velvet lined with Ermine, which was put upon him, then he gave him a Bible, and the Sword was girded on, a Sceptre of Gold given into his hand, and a Speech was made to him, and the Oath given him; Then were great Shouts and the Trumpets sounded, and he sate himselfe downe in the Chair of State, holding the Sceptre in his hand. A Herauld proclaimed his *Title;* The Ceremonie being ended hee went to his Coach, his Traine borne by Mr. *Rich* and other young Nobilitie, so hee hath done his best to come as near to a *Kingship* as might bee.

1657.

There is publicke Advertisement of a Coach drawne by six Horses to sett out from *Aldersgate London*, every Monday to *West-Chester*, also the same to returne every Monday from *Chester;* likewise a Coach and six every Monday to *York*, a great convenience to Travellers.

Nov. 24.

We heare to day that the Ladie *Mary*, as shee is styled, is maried to my Lord *Falconberg*, and her Sister was maried last weeke to Mr. *Rich*, Grandsonne to the Earle of *Warwick:* much worldly Wisdome in his *Highnesse* in procuring these Alliances with men of some ranke for his Familie.

Now is there to bee a new *House* of *Lords;* Writts are issued to divers Persons to sit as Members in the other *House:* wee heare it not called the *House* of *Peers.* It is remarked on this steppe backe to the old Institutions, that if the *Protector* stand in need of the *Lords*, it is like that it will not be long before wee must

Dec. 12.

1657.

Dec. 16,
Wednesday.

have a *King*, and it is thought hee aimes at this Dignitie.

Find Helpe and Comfort in the habit of ejaculatorie Praier, since it is difficult in my present hurried way of life to keepe to my usuall Seasons of retirement during the day: yet doe I strive not to lose hold of my Dependence upon *Divine* Helpe: and so even in Companie or in a Coach, or however occupied, am more content if my Soule hath beene engaged in a short Prayer or Thanksgiving; or if this much is not attained unto, I indeavour to collect my Thoughts, by saying over a Verse or Text that may be applyable to the Businesse wherein I may bee engaged: feele humbled that the cares and vanities of the World take up so much of my time, praie for deliverance from Temptation to Evill, and to be preserved from the more hidden Sinne, the selfe righteous spirit of the *Pharisee*, into which the open wickednesse of others doth oft prove a snare to poore weake human Nature; of myselfe I can do nothing, and may the Faith of St. *Paul* enable me to saie with him, *I can doe all things through Christ who strengtheneth me.*

Dec. 20,
Sunday.

Later than usuall when I arrived at the *Tower:* the striving to keepe a cheerefull

Countenance, and to lighten the Hardships of this long Imprisonment, is beginning to affect my Health: to day my Heart was full, and I gave way, on first meeting my deare *Husband's* embrace, and hidde my Face on his Shoulder, unable to controll my Teares. *My poore Wife, thou art worne out,* he fayd tenderlie, *but cheere up, Love, wee will have a merrie Christmasse yet.* It was very sweet to bee comforted by him, even in a Prison. When the time came that I was to leave, he consented to take into Confideration what I had urged more than once, that I should petition the *Protector* in person.

Yesterday Mr. *Evelyn* and his *Wife* came to *London*, to celebrate *Christmasse-day*, and did prevaile with mee to goe with them to *Exeter Chapell*. Mr. *Gunning* preached on 7 *Micah*, 2 verse. The Sermon ended he did proceed to administer the *Holie Sacrament*, it was then discovered that the Chappell was surrounded with Soldiers; they held their Musketts against us, to the no small feare of some present, yet did they not prevent our going up to the *Altar*. After the Service was finished, those present were made Prisoners, and some carried away. We were of those who did remaine at

1657.

Dec. 26, *Saturday.*

the Houſe. Mr. *Evelyn* did afterward informe us, that after Dinner, of which he was invited to partake, Officers from *Whitehall* came to examine the Priſoners: they queſtioned Mr. *Evelyn* why, contrarie to the ordinance made that the ſuperſtitious Celebration of the *Nativitie* ſhould no longer bee obſerved, hee durſt ſo offend and bee at Common Praiers, which they called *Maſſe* in *Engliſh*; ſo, after much irreverent ſpeaking of this day, and contumeliouſly treating him, they let him goe, content with making this vaine ſhow of their Authoritie.

Lady Willoughby.

1657-8.

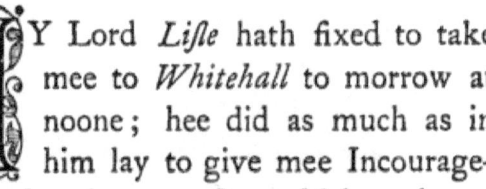

Y Lord *Lisle* hath fixed to take mee to *Whitehall* to morrow at noone; hee did as much as in him lay to give mee Incouragement: felt that the greatest would have beene the more heartie Consent of my *Husband* to this Course: if so bee it faile, the having followed my owne Judgement in putting the matter to this Issue, will adde to my trouble, but this I humbly hope I am prepared to beare; it seemeth cleare to my Minde that we ought not to omitt doing that which on due Consideration and impartially weighing of the subject appeareth to us right, because the Event may hereafter prove us to have misjudged: if wee may not doe Evill that Good may come of it, so wee may not leave undone the Good,

1657-8.

January 8,
Friday.

because it may end in Evill; else wee should sit downe with our Hands before us, and opportunities of Action slide past us, not to bee recalled.

Set forth in a good degree of outward Composure, and not without an inward Strengthening which did greatly support mee; neverthelesse, when wee stopped at *Whitehall*, I had much need of my Lord *Lisle's* arme. When wee entered the Roome, the *Protector* sate at a Table whereon were Papers and Letters. One or two Gentlemen were in attendance, whom hee did dismisse, and then rose. My Lord *Lisle* spake a few Wordes and ledde me towards him: He bowed as I advanced, with the Petition held in my hand, and presented it to him; he tooke it, and motioned to mee to be seated. I was faine to obey him through Weaknesse, else would it have better pleased mee not to accept even this small Courtisie at his hands. He glanced at the Paper and then spake: *The Lord Willoughby doth intreat his Enlargement in a more humble tone it seems, as does better suit his Condition, and doth no longer talke high of Injustice and the like: it is well; He is one who, having set his hand to the Plough, hath turned backe, and concerning such is it not sayd they are accurfed? what fayeth the Spirrit to the* Laodiceans? *For that thou art neither cold nor hot, I will fpew thee out of my Mouth.* He went on in this manner for fome time, and then fayd, *I doe perceave my Lord* Willoughby *giveth us his word that, fo hee may bee allowed to goe forth for a fpace, to attend to the needfull Settlement of his Affaires, he will returne to his Imprifonment. But how expeƈteth hee to bee beleeved; Who fhall put their truft in fuch as he?* Hereat I fpake with fome warmth, *May I reminde your* Highneffe *that you fpeake to the Lord* Willoughby's *Wife, and ill would it become her to heare fuch Wordes unmoved. I crave your* Highneffe's *pardon, but meethinks no Aƈt of my* Lorde *doth warrant any Man, much leffe your* Highneffe, *to doubt his Honour. You fhall judge yourfelfe,* Madam, he replied; thereupon hee turned to a Cabinet that was neare to him, and tooke out fome Papers; from thefe hee did feleƈt two Letters, one of thefe hee unfolded and afked mee did I know the writing? I could not denie that I did; there was no fignature, and the latter part was in Cyphers. *That is not the onely one,* he continued, and opened another, and gave it mee, dated but two months backe: His *Highneffe* did then commence a Difcourfe,

1657-8. if so it could be called, seeming rather a somewhat confused utterance of his Thoughts; quoting sundrie Texts of *Scripture*, which he did intersperse with talke of Governement, High-treason, and so forth: of some men beeing forced against their Will, to rule the State, though sorely oppressed by the Burthen: this seemingly addressed to other ears than mine; after a while hee paused, and I againe spoke something in this manner, that I did conceeve a Prisoner and one illegally made so, had a full right to use any means in his power to escape, and to engage his Friends in his behalf. As he replyed not, I further sayd, *If your* Highnesse *cast your eye backe a few yeares, it would be seene that the Lord* Willoughby *did show as true concernment for the Libertie of the Nation, as others who were then striving onely to obtaine this Justice for the People ; That hee beleeveing that howsoever righteous a Cause might bee, that it would not sanctifie un-righteous Meanes, and foreseeing great Evill and Confusion, did stop short in the Worke, was no dishonour to him as a Christian or a Gentleman. As to High Treason, it passeth my poore abilitie to comprehend what doth make High Treason, seeing it changeth sides with the strongest, and is the Crime of the*

Lady Willoughby.

Oppreffed refifting the Oppreffor. I marvell that I fpake fo boldly. So I arofe and fayd, *Since Your* Highneffe *fetteth at nought my* Lord's *Word, your* Highneffe's *Anfwer will bee beft tranfmitted through your Secretarie, a* Wife's *Lippes repeate not Words of fuch indignitie to her* Hufband, *I begge your* Highneffe's *leave to withdraw.* To my furprife he did detain mee, and queftioned mee on fome indifferent and trifling Matters, as it appeared to mee, then of a fudden changed his Tone, faying, *Who can find a vertuous Woman? her Price is far above Rubies, the Heart of her* Hufband *doth fafely truft in her.* Madam, we doe accept my Lord Willoughby's *Termes,* holding his *Wife's* truth as his hoftage, his Petition fhall be laid before the Councill. So ended the Interview, and I hafted to the *Tower.* It is rumoured that the *Protector* is greatly defirous that the old *Peeres* fhould come to his new *Houfe* of *Lords;* hence his wifh to conciliate in fome Quarters. His Lookes are not thofe of one at eafe in his Pofition, his Face was worne and caft-downe, and I obferved an anxious manner of liftening to any Sound, and once at a fudden movement of my Lord *Lifle,* he ftarted and looked behind him, feeming as though hee would have put his Hand on the Piſtolls which were beſide him, but checked himſelfe; doe compaſſionate him, as one who hath felt himſelfe called to a mightie Worke, the Iſſues whereof have beene too mightie for his Guidance, and too full of Temptation and Conflict for his Peace. Many do ſay of him, that never was there a man of ſo great Courage and Abilitie to lead others. With Power have come Pride and Selfe-exaltation, and theſe have brought Crueltie, and Injuſtice: but who am I that I ſhould judge him, or ſpeake of events above my Knowledge and Place; Let mee be thankfull for the proſpect of the ſpeedie Releaſe of my beloved *Huſband* from his long Impriſonment.

Jan. 9, Saturday. Tooke a Coach and went to *Weſtminſter*, and waited at my Kinſman's till a Friend came in from the *Houſe*, and brought me the comforting Newes that an Order had been paſſ'd that the Lord *Willoughby* of *Parham* ſhall be diſcharg'd of his Impriſonment, upon his Honour, and upon the Engagement in 10 Thouſand Pounds of his Friends, that hee ſhall peaceably demeane himſelfe for the future, and ſhall not join with or have any Correſpondence with any Enemies of the *Lord Protector* &c. Wedneſday the 10th of January appointed for the Priſoner

Lady Willoughby.

to bee brought to the *Bar* of the *Houſe*; *William Willoughby* tooke word to the *Tower*, the while I went with *Fanny* to looke for another and more commodious Lodging, that we now have, not being ſuitable to my *Lord*. Found one in *Queen Street*, handſomely furniſhed and provided, the People of the houſe civillie inclined.

Jan. 12, Tueſday. — My deare Life in excellent ſpirits, and divers of our Friends came to ſuppe with us; did, by mutuall conſent, ſpeake little of either *King* or *Protector*, this being ſo joyfull an occaſion.

Jan. 20, Wedneſday. — The *Houſe* of *Commons* met this day, as alſo the new *Houſe* of *Lords*; none of the old, ſave one or two, would ſit with this medley of perſons ſummoned by the *Protector*. Even the Earl of *Warwick* kept out of the way. It is ſayd the *Protector* is greatly caſt downe in private, and is at his Wits' end for Money. Truely, this hath an aire of *Royaltie*.

Find wee cannot leave *London* at preſent. Our excellent friend Mr. *Evelyn* hath not been abroad of late, by reaſon of the illneſſe of his Son *Richard*, who hath the Ague; Fanny is in much concerne for him, ſhee hath oft deſcribed him as a Child of rare beautie and endowment.

January 28, Thurſday. — Arrived a meſſage from *Sayes Court*. The poore *Child* died yeſter-day.

1657-8.
Feb. 5.

Great sensation caused by the sudden, and most unexpected, dissolving of *Parliament*, they having sate but a Fortnight. The *Protector* hath mett with vexatious Opposition in the *House* of *Commons*, who take no account of the upper *House* which hee hath lately raised up; and it is supposed that this, and some private cause of Displeasure, and secret Information of the *Royalists* movements, did so worke on him, hee beeing also ill in Health, that in some sudden heat and distemperature, hee hurried to the *House*, waiting not for his Carriage, but, calling his Guards, tooke a Coach standing neare *Whitehall*, and so went downe, and sent for the *Commons*, who adjourning their Businesse did follow the Usher into his presence. He accused them of some being leagued with *Charles Stuart*, and others of disturbing the People with a talke of devising the *Commonwealth* anew, and so falling off from their former Advice and Petition to him; seeing this to bee the end of their sitting, he did dissolve that *Parliament*. These Particulars I have thought it worth while here to sett downe, as I did hear them given yester-night to my *Lord* by one present. During the day, many coming and going. Came to dine with us, my Lord

Lady Willoughby.

Baltimore; a lively Discourse was carried on, the Conversation turned chiefely to the state of the Colonies, a subject of interest to my *Husband;* and my Lord *Baltimore* entered into a more particular Relation of the early Settlement of *Maryland* by his Father, Sir George Calvert, who did consider that entire libertie of Conscience in matters of Religion, was the true foundation of Prosperity and Happinesse of a People, and did make Laws to this effect: that no one in his Colony should be hindered or molested in the exercise of his Religion. This liberality of Sentiment the more commendable in him, that he was a *Papist.* And so it was that his Colony did flourish exceedingly for some years. But of late it has fallen into the hands of others, under this present Government, who have excluded all Roman Catholicks from the benefit of the wise and benevolent Laws of their Founder, and brought Discord and Strife into the Settlement. So it seemeth the *Saviour's* words must come to pass, and men make his Religion of Love a cause of Hatred and Uncharitablenesse. Will it ever be on Earth that the Tree of Life shall spread forth its Branches, and *its Leaves be for the healing of the Nations?*

My Lord *Brereton* hath writt to my *Husband*

1657-8.

Feb. 15,
Monday.

at the requeſt of his Sonne; the Engagement of the young People hath beene ſo informally entered into, that we felt it to bee our Dutie to requeſt ſome explanation. Mr. *Brereton* did unadviſedly yield himſelfe to the Captivation of *our incomparable Daughter*, ſo doth his Father ſtyle her, unmindfull of the Conſequence, and hath by ſweet intelligence of Lookes, and more ſweet muſicke of low dropping Wordes, and interchange of Thought in all deare Friendſhip and pure Affection, ſo tuned her Heart to his, that either apart knoweth but a ſad monotony, now hee is like one diſtracted, having but a poore Purſe, and neither Houſe nor Land whereon to make claime to our favour; his Father's propertie is involved, as that of ſo manie other of the *King's* Friends, in the Misfortunes of the times, and my Lord *Brereton* would confer with my *Huſband* on this matter, and doth propoſe to call at our Lodging to morrow at 10 of the Clocke.

Feb. 17, Wedneſday.

Since the publication of a Pamphlet, entitled, *Killing no Murder*, the *Protector* hath become ſo ſuſpicious of Treacherie as is pitiable to heare of. It is ſay'd he hath of late made the rounds of the poſts at *Whitehall* in Perſon, and doth continually change his ſleeping Roome. He

Lady Willoughby.

1657-8.

difmiffed not long time ago his moft faithfull Guards and Officers, and for fome while paft hath worne Piftolls concealed in his Dreffe; one that knew his *Mother* did affure mee her Death was haftened by her perpetuall feare for his Life, fhee would ftart at the firing of a Mufket, and was ill at eafe if fhee faw not her Sonne every day, to be certified of his Safetie.

No marvel that he is confcience-ftricken, who hardened his Heart to the cries of the *Irifh* People, and was the flayer of Thoufands, defenceleffe Men, Women and Children, men in the *Sanctuarie*, whither they had fled for fafetie; who did caufe wretched Families to be torne from their homes and fold in the Plantations: and fold for Slaves his fellow Countreymen, whom the chances of Warre left Prifoners in his hand. Neverthelesse men faye, in his fanatick notions of faving Grace, hee cafteth a Cloke over all his Sinnes; the day hath beene that he would have fay'd *Is thy Servant a Dog that he fhould doe this thing?*

Feb. 27, *Saturday.*

Mr. *Evelyn* called: at his departure left with us a Paper containing a fhort Memoriall of his little Sonne.

March 3, *Wednefday.*

Died, laft moneth, Mr. *Rich* the *Protector's* Sonne-in-law.

1657-8.
March 4,
Thurſday.

The Cold continues very ſharp, the Winde northerly, no hope of change. One paſſing neare the little Turne-ſtyle in *Holborn*, ſaw two Boyes of the Prieſt's Schoole feeding or endeavouring to feed a ſtarved Crow, which was frozen by the Feet to its Prey; it flapped its Wings feebly now and then, and preſently died.

May 15,
Saturday.

Heare my Lord *Winchelſea* is about to be maried againe; have reaſon to thinke it not unlikely and ſee no offence to us: my poore *Daughter* left no *Children*, and the Earle did lament her Death as much as was in his nature; and as hee had found Contentment in the maried ſtate, ſo there may not bee imputed to him diſreſpect to her Memorie if hee againe ſeeke, although it be ſomewhat haſtily, the enlivening Societie and Comfort of a Wife.

My deare *Life* left *London* this day, hee having preſſing Buſineſſe both at *Parham* and in *Lincolnſhire*; and it ſeemed beſt that I ſhould remaine here.

Some Paſſages copied from Mr. *Evelyn's* Memoriall of His Sonne, he having given me permiſſion.

" Jan. 27. After ſix fits of a Quartaine Ague
" with which it pleaſed God to viſite him, died

"my deare Sonne *Richard*, to our inexpreffible
"Griefe and Affliction, 5 yeares and 3 days
"onely, but at that tender Age a Prodigie for
"Wit and Underftanding; for Beautie of
"Bodie a very Angel; for endowment of
"Minde, of incredible and rare hopes. To
"give onely a little tafte of fome of them and
"thereby Glorie to *God*, who out of the
"mouthes of Babes and Infantes does fome-
"times perfect his Praifes; at 2 yeares and a
"halfe old he could perfectly reade any of the
"*Englifh*, *Latine*, *French*, or *Gothic* letters,
"pronouncing the three firft Languages ex-
"actly. He had before the 5th yeare, or in
"that yeare, not onely fkill to reade moft
"written hands, but to decline all the Nounes,
"conjugate Verbes &c.; began himfelfe to
"write legibly and had a ftrong paffion for
"*Greeke*. Strange was his apt and ingenious
"application of Fables and Moralls, for he
"had read *Æfop*: he had a wonderfull difpo-
"fition to Mathematicks, having by heart
"divers Propofitions of *Euclid* that were read
"to him in play, and he would make Lines
"and demonftrate them. As to his Pietie,
"aftonifhing were his applications of *Scripture*
"upon occafion, and his fenfe of *God*: hee

1658.

"had learn'd all his Catechifme early, and
"underftood that part of the *Bible* and *New*
"*Teftament* to a wonder, how *Chrift* came to
"redeeme Mankind, and how, comprehending
"thefe neceffaries himfelfe, his *Godfathers* were
"difcharged of their Promife. Thefe and the
"like illuminations far exceeding his Age and
"Experience, confidering the prettineffe of his
"Addreffe and Behaviour, cannot but leave
"impreffion in mee at the memorie of him.
"Often hee would defire thofe who came to
"fee him, to praie by him, and a yeare before
"he fell ficke, to kneele and praie alone with
"him in fome corner.

"How thankfully would he receive Admo-
"nition, how foone be reconciled! how in-
"different yet continually cheerefull! He was
"all life, all prettineffe, far from morofe, fullen
"or childifh, in anything hee faid or did.
"The laft time hee had beene at Church, I
"afked him according to cuftome what he re-
"membered of the Sermone. Two good
"things, Father, faid hee, *bonum gratiæ* and
"*bonum gloriæ*. The day before hee died he
"call'd to me and told mee that for all I loved
"him fo dearly, I fhould give my Houfe,
"Land, and all my fine things to his Brother

" *Jacke*, he fhould have none of them: and
" next morning, when he found himfelfe ill,
" and that I perfuaded him to keepe his Hands
" in bed, he demanded whether hee might
" praie to *God* with his Hands unjoyned; and
" a little after, whilft in great Agonie, whether
" hee fhould not offend *God* by ufing his holie
" Name fo often, calling for eafe. So earlie
" Knowledge, fo much Pietie and Perfection!
" But thus *God*, having dreffed up a Saint fit
" for himfelfe, would not longer permitt him
" with us, unworthie of the future Fruites of
" this incomparable hopefull Bloffome. Such
" a Child I never faw: for fuch a Child I bleffe
" God in whofe bofome hee is! May I and
" mine become as this little Child. Thou
" gaveft him to us, Thou haft taken him from
" us, bleffed be the name of the *Lord*. That
" I had anything acceptable to Thee was from
" Thy grace alone, fince from mee he had
" nothing but Sinne, but that thou haft par-
" doned! bleffed be *God* for ever. *Amen.*"

Mr. *Evelyn* doth intend to infert fome fhort Hiftorie of his Sonne in a Booke he is about to print, entituled, *Golden Booke of St.* Chryfoftome *concerning the Education of Children.*

1658.
May 19,
Wednesday.

May 20,
Thursday.

Fanny is pale, and cast downe; wish I could give her Comfort, but cannot as yet.

Conversation with my Lord *Brereton*: like him for the kind Manner with which hee entereth into his Sonnes Difficulties, and his readinesse to make any Sacrifice on his part, esteeming his Sonne most fortunate and himselfe honoured by an Alliance with our Familie. Hee and my *Lord*, after frequent deliberation, do now entertaine the hope that some sort of suitable Provision may bee made, that may tend to the Accomplishment of the Mariage sooner than at first did appeare could bee with prudence. Mr. *Brereton* received from my *Husband* a few Wordes of reproofe, not unmerited yet leniently administered, on the part he had acted, seeing that no man doth transplant a faire Rose Tree from the Garden where it grew, lovingly nourished, and carefully tended, untill he hath first made readie a fitting Shelter.

May 24,
Monday.

To day as Mr. *Brereton* came up to mee to hand me to the Coach, he did expresse in lively terms his sense of the Favour conferred upon him, and then, respectfully taking my Hand and pressing it to his Lippes, he did beseech mee to accept his dutifull Affection and to beleeve that nought could so adde to his already great Happineſſe, as to bee a Sonne to mee in the place of him whoſe untimely Loſſe he knew I did yet mourne; it was kindly ſayd, and his young Face ſpake more than Wordes.

Aug. 21, Saturday.

Parted from my deare *Daughter* ; may the bleſſing of *God* be upon her! in *his bleſſing may her Houſe bee bleſſed*. And may hee who hath ſought from us this precious Gift, prove worthie of her! We can ill ſpare her, as hee will ill deſerve her if he bee not faithfull to his Truſt; not that I doubt his concerne for her Happineſs, but it needeth much to outweigh the Feares that do naturally ariſe. Time will doubtleſſe reconcile mee to my Loſſe.

Aug. 23, Monday.

Have with pleaſure obſerved that Mr. *Brereton* hath leſſe of ſelfe ſeeking than moſt men; he has a ſingleneſſe of Heart that ſeeketh firſt the Happineſſe of others: alſo outwardly he hath much to commend him in the graces of his Perſon and noble Carriage; he is a Gentleman of a ſweet diſpoſition, yet altogether manly; his Manners gentle and courteous, yet not deficient in Dignitie; well accompliſhed and learned, and of excellent Vertue. He is ſilent, and when hee ſpeaketh it is in few Wordes; yet this not from conſtraint, or feare of others; free from all ſervile deſire to pleaſe, ſo hath he

1658.

no feare of offending any; nor yet from povertie of Thought, but is rather one who may say,

> *My Minde to me a Kingdome is,*
> *Such perfect Joy therein I find.*

Thus I doe endeavour to set forth the Excellencies of this young Man, that in so doing my deare *Child's* gaine may bee advantaged in my eyes, and our Losse bee the more cheerefully borne; it seemeth as though Faith were weakest for those whom we most love. Gave my sweet *Daughter* a Paper containing a feeble attempt to give utterance, to the Love and Solicitude of manie yeares. At this time I am not without Trouble and that of a sort wherewith I am well acquainted; my deare *Husband* takes ill the Conditions wherein he is allowed his Libertie: all Parties are scheming and prophecying, and he under a Bond to keep quiet, to him at no time an easie matter, is under continual liabilitie of suspition from the Conduct of others who do desire to draw him into their Plots and Devices.

August 24, Tuesday.

Low in Bodie and Spirrit yet not dismayed. A kind of apprehensivenesse not usual with mee cometh over mee, as I looke at the only *Child* left mee, as if some unseene Danger threatened her. Shee, though shee too hath losse in her Sister's Marriage, seeth no Clowde, and is all gaietie and full of Merriment with her young Kinsfolk.

Since the Death of his *Daughter*, at which time hee lay ill of the Gout, the *Protector's* Health has failed more and more. The Lady *Claypole* did vainely intreate for the life of Dr. *Hewet*: she had sate under his Ministrie, and did hold him in great esteeme; the *Protector*, who had a more than ordinarie Affection for his *Daughter*, was sorely besett, and shee so ill: yet would he not yeeld to her Entreatie, and did onely remit the Sentence that he be hanged, &c. and allowed him to be beheaded. This small mercie was likewise extended to Sir *Henry Slingsby*: the other Prisoners, it may be here mentioned, who were concerned in that Plot, Mr. *Russell*, Sir *William Compton*, and others, did escape; my *Husband* was freed from all suspition of being connected with it, the conditions of his Freedome beeing well knowne; and he had in truth devoted himselfe to his private Affaires, which did stand in much need of Settlement. The *Protector* did remaine at *Hampton Court*, during the last Illnesse of his Daughter, whose sufferings were

1658.

August 25, *Wednesday*.

1658.

very great: It was fayd he came oft to her bed fide, performing, as far as his own paine and ficknefſe would permit, the laſt ſad Offices, until ſhe was releaſed; ſmoothing her Pillow, giving her Medicines and Cordials with his own Hand; miniſtering to her Wants, with all gentleneſs and affection. She deceaſed the 6th of Auguſt. Hee is now very ill; his Diſeaſe is underſtood to be a Tertian Ague, and hee is confined to his Bed. Some that are well informed, ſay, that hee hath declared to his Wife and Familie, that he is well aſſured that hee ſhall not die at this time.

Aug. 26, Thurſday.

His *Highneſs's* ficknefſe encreaſeth; hee was yeſterday removed to *Whitehall* for change of Aire, but is no better; an expreſſe Meſſenger is ſent to his Sonne *Henry* in *Ireland*.

Aug. 29, Sunday.

The fits of the *Ague* do ſo encreaſe that the report at *Whitehall* to day, is, that his *Highneſſe* is ſcarce ever free from them, the *Phyſitians* yet hope hee may ſtruggle through; Praiers are dayly put up for him, as one of his Friends was heard to ſay, *Never was there a greater ſtocke of praiers going for any man than is now going for him.*

Sept. 1, Wedneſday.

When my Lord *Say* left *Whitehall* this fore-noone, the *Protector* was at that time delirious.

Lady Willoughby.

1658.

It is supposed that there are frequent private Meetings of the *King's* friends: they found their cheife Hopes on the Divisions like to bee in the other Partie; some say the Succession is appointed, others that a Paper, thought to bee the *Protector's* Will, the which hee sent for when at *Hampton Court* when his illnesse did become so formidable, was not to bee found, and so his Sonnes Succession will be disputed. The Countrey will be throwne, it is to be feared, into Confusion and Strife. May the *Lord* have mercie upon this poore People and save us from the horrors of another Warre. My deare *Life* hath ridde up with all speed to *London*.

Sept. 2, Thursday.

Mr. *Evelyn* has just called, my Lord *Lisle*, Mr. *Pepys*, and divers others: no one knows what to expect. Mr. *Evelyn* had mett a Friend in the Street, who had heard from one who was come from the *Palace*, and had spoken to a Gentleman just forth the sicke Roome, that the *Protector* was more himselfe: His *Highnesse* spake to those neare his Bed, and called on one of his Chaplaines to reade a Text from the Bible that he named, to him, and in a manner very affecting made some Remarke thereon, and afterward did praie devoutly and humbly.

1658.

Sept. 3, Friday.

So awfull hath beene this Day, and the laſt Night, that I feele ſcarce able to guide the Penne. It is all over, the *Protector* is no more; on this day that he hath ever conſidered his fortunate Day. His *Highneſſe* had ſunke into a kind of Stupor, after the interval of conſciouſneſſe yeſternoone, but revived a little in the night-time, and did utter a few Wordes, ſaying, *God is good, hee will not leave mee.*

He was reſtleſſe moſt part of the Night, ſpeaking to himſelfe in broken Sentences; after, hee appeared unconſcious, though ſtill breathing, and ſo did continue till his Spiritt was releaſed in the Afternoone, at 4 of the clock. During the Night was there ſuch a Storme as I never remember: People were frighted out of their beds, Houſes ſhooke as they would fall, and the Sound of the Wind was terrible to heare: but the dying Man heard it not. Every one that cometh in has to tell of new Diſaſter: Roofes carried off, Chimnies blowne downe, and great Trees in the Parks torne up by the Roots; manie of the Linden Trees at the Lord Treaſurer's in the *Strand* are broken off.

Lady Willoughby.

1662.

Letter from the Lord *Willoughby* to his *Wife*.

Deare Heart,

Aving occasion to send *Lydgate* into the Countrey on some Businesse of a nature not to be entrusted to Paper, I at the same time make him Bearer of these Lines to my deare *Wife*, whose tender Heart will suffer in that I have to write. This afternoone was sent out of the World the honestest and noblest Man in it: Sir *Harry Vane* was beheaded on *Tower Hill*, notwithstanding that his *Majestie* had pledged his word to remitt the Sentence, should it be given against him, which it was knowne the *Soliciter Generall* had resolved: there is a Curse methinks on Kingship; and the Royall Word is ever to be a Mockerie. There

1662.

was assembled a vast Multitude, numbers at Windowes and on the tops of the Houses: as Sir *Harry* pass'd within the *Tower* railing, the acclamations of the People were loud, manie crying out, *The Lord goe with you, The Lord helpe you.* He did make acknowledgement by taking off his Hat at different times: as the Sled was drawne slowly through the Crowd, I heard one who stood neere the Sled, say to him, it was the most glorious Seat he had ever sate in; he answered him, *It is indeed;* one man who had knowne him in *New England*, pressed forward to bid *God* blesse him, the Teares on his furrowed Face. As he stood on the Scaffold the multitude were strucke with Admiration at his noble Presence as hee began to speake to them: but he was presently interrupted by Sir *John Robinson*, who was there for this intent, and who ordered the Trumpeters to come neare, and sound the Trumpets before his Face, to prevent his being heard, and this was done severall times, and his Notes were rudely snatched from his Hands as I am credibly informed, but did not see it; the People were much moved by what he say'd, and it was feared they might be wrought upon in a degree like to be dangerous, if he was permitted to go on with his Difcourfe. As he knelt downe, one that was neare heard one or two fhort Sentences, fuch as, *I bleffe the Lord who hath counted me worthie to fuffer for his Name. I bleffe the Lord I have not deferted the righteous Caufe for which I fuffer.* Such, deare *Wife*, was the end of this good and upright Man. As the People went their way after the fatal Stroke was given, there was much murmuring: they fpake one to another of his manifold Vertues, his integritie in Office; while fome fcrupled not fcoffingly to jeft on the worth of a Kings Promife, and others, whofe Garb betokened them of fomewhat better Rank than the crowd, did with great warmth enlarge on that Speech of his in the *Houfe* fome while ago, when he did fupport the Petition of the Royalifts, Prifoners fold for Slaves in the publicke Market at *Barbadoes* by order of the *Protector*. His *Majeftie* is blamed by many. I mett Mr. *Pepys*, who had witneffed the Execution, and hee fayd to mee, the *King* would lofe more by this Man's Death than he would get againe for a good while. Tho' of late differing from Sir *Harry Vane*, there had beene no perfonall Enmitie betweene us, and greatly defiring, in remembrance of our former Friendfhip, to fee him once more, in companie with others of his Friends, I viſited him on the morning of his Death. *Why*, ſay'd hee, *ſhould wee bee affrighted with Death? I bleſſe the Lord I am ſo farre from being affrighted with Death, that I find it rather ſhrinke from mee than I from it.* Kiſſing his Children he gave them his Bleſſing, ſaying, the *Lord* would be to them a better Father than he was: told them not to be troubled for him, he was going home to his Father. I have writt theſe particulars for your private reading. Farewell, ſweet *Wife*, whom I dearly love, yet would I rather be the dead Sir *Harry Vane*, than one who muſt be nameleſſe.

Willoughby.

Strand,
This 14th day of *June* 1662.

1663.

Ind as I grow older encreafing reluctancy to take up my Penne; it may be that I am leffe moved than formerly by publick Events and Circumftances, and more difpofed to wait for the end, wherein if we patiently wait, will be made manifeft the purpofes of the Divine Government; alfo I am led to beleeve that it is fafer for mee to looke to prefent Duties without looking backeward or forward, which doth ofttimes diftract the Minde or overweigh the Spirit with more care or trouble than doth of right belong to the time being. Taking by chance out of my writing Drawer this little booke in which are infcribed many Paffages of my paft Life and Experiences, I did open it and read fome; and feeing that for nigh four Yeares nothing hath beene added thereto, for the fake

1663.

of my deare *Daughters*, who hereafter may not unlikely peruse this Memoriall of their *Mother*, I will endeavour shortly to fill up the space to this time, and this under some degree of solemn feeling that when these Wordes are read by them I shall be no more in this Life, but have passed to Judgement. And here it seemeth to mee, not out of Season to exhort you, my beloved Children, to remember, that such as ye are made by the discipline of Time, such ye will be when Death opens the Doore and ye passe into Eternity. During these few Yeares great changes have been wrought in Publick Affaires. The sudden Death of the late *Protector* was followed by anarchie and confusion; his Sonne was speedily and quietly set aside: the Republican Partie were for a while uppermost, and they re-called the old Members, who had been excluded from the *House of Commons*, and strove to build up a similitude of the old notion of a Common wealth, but there was Division and Weaknesse: some abandoned the Scheme, and imagined to bring back the Monarchie under restrictions that should so limit the prerogative of the Crown, as to keepe a just Ballance, and since it was sayed, so many were for a King, why should it not bee the rightfull

Heir to the Throne? Others fayed, they objected not to a King, but would not have a Catholicke, which would bee to perill the reformed Religion and the Libertie for which they had fought and ftriven: my deare *Hufband* did moftly agree with thofe who would reftore the exiled *Monarch*, and did privately conferre with Sir *Bulftrode Whitelocke*, General *Fleetwood*, and a few others. But whether they moved too flowly, or differed in opinion how to act, I know not: *Whitelocke* was threatened with Imprifonment, and betooke himfelfe to the Countrey, to be out of the way, leaveing the *Great Seale* with his *Wife*, to be delivered to the *Speaker*. So it was for a time, that the Nation might be fayd to have no Government. My Lord, when he did perceive that nothing was to be done in that direction, joyned the *Royalifts* and did fupply them with Money to buy Arms. Then it was agreed that a Rifing fhould be on a day fixed in July; it was in the yeare 1659. My *Hufband*, in conjunction with Sir *Horatio Townfend*, was to take poffeffion of *Lyn*; Sir *George Booth* iffued a Proclamation in the North, calling upon the People to aid in forming a fettled Government, yet not nameing the *King ;* but it appeared that the Plott had beene

1663.

discovered, a letter of the Lady *Mary Howard* was intercepted, and she was arrested; and presently my *Husband*, Sir *George Booth*, Sir *William Compton*, also I thinke the Earle of *Stamford*, Collonel *Rossiter*, were all taken, and sent to the *Tower*. I heard one say afterward, that the Lord *Willoughby* did make very merrie as he once more entered his former Abode. It is farre beyond my poore Abilitie to set downe the state of the Countrie and different parts taken by those severally concerned; I beleeve manie were sore discomforted and under great discouragement and had no hearte to stirre in the confused state of Affaires, the *Parliament* and the *Armie* were at continuall strife, and each divided within itselfe.

Aug. 24, Monday.

So at last the *Armie* in the north with Generall *Monck*, he now Duke of *Albemarle*, at their head came to *London*. Some sayd he was for raising himselfe to be *Protector*, others that he was for the *King*. General *Lambert* was sent to the *Tower*. And here I may stop to mention that by meanes of a long Rope, he, like the Apostle, let himselfe downe the Wall at some height, and was received into a Boate underneath the Windore, whereat he got out; but hee, poore Man, not content to lie concealed, was shortly re-taken and brought back to Prison. Generall *Monck* appeared at the first to seeke the favour of *Parliament*, and did yield himselfe to the bidding of the Leaders; then some Act did displease the *Citie*, and he turned that way: in time the Truth came out, that he was secretly at worke for the *King*. They who did beare rule in the *House of Commons*, did now cause Sir *Harry Vane* to bee put under Arrest, and kept in durance at *Belleau*, his House in *Lincolnshire*. The same were well disposed to some others, so were set at Libertie my deare *Husband* after a short Captivitie, Sir *George Booth*, and their Friends. The end came at last of this mis-rule and disturbed Course, a Messenger arrived from *Breda*, who appeared at the doore of the *House* and did make request to speake to the *Lord General*, to whom he presented a Letter, which no doubt was expected by *Monck*. Afterward he was called in, and did then deliver up Letters addressed to the two *Houses*, and also a Paper which did contain the Promise of a free and generall Pardon, and Libertie of Conscience in Religion. Then it was moved that a Letter should be writt inviting the *King* to returne, likewise a present of Money for himselfe and his Brother, greatly needed. Some, more pru-

1663.

1663.

dent than others, would have stayed these hasty Proceedings, in order to stipulate certaine Conditions, but the *Lord Generall* did overrule the matter, saying, it would be time enough afterward: which haste was to be repented of, as doth now unhappily appeare, men hurried to the overthrow of their own Worke.

In a little while the King entered London amid great rejoycings, and acclamations of the People.

It needeth not to particularize more, neither may it be altogether expedient: Persecutions, Imprisonment, and Death are on all sides, on the score of Religion, no lesse than of Revenge for the death of the late King. The Execution of Sir *Harry Vane* strucke to the heart of his Friends, and was condemned by his Enemies. A yeare ago, or thereabout, his Majestie married the Infanta of *Portugal*, who hath her Confessor and Private Chappel, where the Masse is celebrated.

August 26, Wednesday.

To leave publick Affaires—Our excellent friend Mr. *Evelyn* is much noticed at Court; he is well pleased that his Majestie hath given his Countenance to the Society which he and Mr. *Robert Boyle*, and other learned and ingenious men, so long ago devised and assembled together. Also he hath receaved Prayse and Commendation of his Booke entituled, *Sylva*, or a discourse on Trees, from the King himself as well as others.

Have lately given in marriage our beloved Daughter *Elizabeth* to Mr. *Jones*, the eldest Sonne of my Lord *Ranelagh*. Doe live in much Retirement; having a naturall inclination for Solitude, it pleaseth me well: but my deare *Husband* hath but little aptitude for a quiett Life, and doth speake of again visiting *Barbadoes* and *Antigua*, and this with more seriousnesse of purpose since he hath heard from his Friends, that his *Majestie* would likely make him *Governor* of the *Islands*.

Lady *Ranelagh* is the deare and much esteemed Friend of Mr. *Evelyn* and his *Wife*, and *Sister* to Mr. *Robert Boyle*, who hath for her a more than common Affection, and hath had a Picture of her painted in Oyle. I thought not so soone to be called upon to give up the last Lamb of my little Flock, whom I would faine have kept by my side yet a little while, and this not for my owne sake alone. She may I feare mee have to live in *Ireland*, and hath beene somewhat too delicately nurtured to beare the Hardships that shee may have to encounter, yet hath shee a Sprightlinesse and Vivacitie of Disposition not prone to magnifie Trouble, and

1663.

ſtill leſſe to ſeeke it; and ſo farre is fitted to take Life bravely. Oft I have thought her moſt like unto a little merrie Bird, and now ſhee too is gone from mee. How greatly have I been favoured in my Children, "*pretie Playfellows*" in my youth, dutiful Daughters, and deare Companions, the Joy and Comfort of my advancing Years. The houſe would be emptie and ſilent were it not for the ſound of little Footſteppes of more than one Grandchild and the happie Voices of their Parents.

Aug. 27, Thurſday.

Wearied and ſomewhat ſad at Heart, I lay'd down my Penne yeſterday, and ſhortly afterward was ſent for to give ſome helpe to one of our poore Neighbours. The Leſſon came not amiſſe, and the Worde of the Diſciple to the blind Man, came to my remembrance, *Be of good Comfort, ariſe, hee calleth thee*. There was ſtill Worke for mee to doe: beleave we doe not ſufficiently take Comfort in this, that it is He who calleth us; howſoever ſmall may appeare the Dutie, or lowly the Service. Late in the Afternoone as I ſate in the Windore at the eaſt end of the long Gallerie, there fell a heavy Shower of Rain; on a ſudden the Sun ſhone out brightly, and above the Wood oppoſite, a Rainebow reaching acroſſe to the upland Field of Corn Sheaves; it did remind mee of my beloved *Mother*, of her readineſſe to draw forth the ſacred Teaching contained in the great Booke of Nature, and I remembered the Day when wee ſtood together at that ſame Windore, and I was very ſorrowfull, and there did appeare to us then as now, the manie coloured Rainebow midſt the falling Drops, ſhe looked wiſtfully at my ſad Countenance as ſhee ſay'd, Deare Child, this beautifull Emblem as it is made viſible to us onely in the falling Raine, ſo is it not in the viſitations of Sorrow that the Heart is gladdened by the ſweeteſt Tokens of God's Love? Sorrow from His Hand hath ever Sweetneſſe mingled therewith, it melteth the Heart, which doth more readily yeeld itſelf to the Divine Will, to be as Clay in the hands of the Potter. Thus, or in like Wordes, ſhee ſpake. How great have beene my Priviledges, much hath beene given, much will be required.

It hath beene permitted mee to feele as Yeares increaſe, Faith ſtrengthened, ſpirituall Perceptions quickened, and ſpirituall Diſcernment enlarged; praiſed be *God*, in whom is all fulneſſe of Knowledge, Grace and Truth.

Buſied this Forenoone in ordering ſome

1663.

changes in the Houfehold: looked over the Linnen and made out a Lift of fome that could bee fpared for my daughter *Brereton;* in the toppe of the Linnen Cheft found one or two of my firft Babie-cloathes ftrewed with Lavender, carefully pinned up and put away by poore old Nurfe; tooke up the lace Cap, the two who had worne it firft, my little Sonne my precious *William*, and my beloved Daughter *Diana,* both taken. Can I now fay *It is well?* all things vifible will paffe away, but the unfeene will remaine, fo if the Heart loveth thefe, its Treafures are fafe in Heaven. When evening came I walked forth; the Sunne had gone down behind *Framlingham,* leaving a bright golden Edge upon the narrow ridge of darke Cloud; the Aire was foft and the Gilloflowers on the low Wall gave out a pleafant Perfume as I paffed; ftopped and pluckt fome of the pale yellow Flowers as I thought of the day whereon my three little Maidens brought the young Plants from the Caftle, and planted them here, the while I ftood bye looking at their happie Faces; now one is not, and the others are farre from mee. As I walked to & fro on the Terrace faw the Rookes as they flowly winged their way over head to their Nefts;

how small a thing maketh the full Cup to overflow, the Tears rose to my Eyes, my home was deserted. As it became darker the Starres, which did at first show but dimly, were now bright and sparkling; There was scarce a sound, the Birds were all silent, save the Owl in the farre wood; a Bat flitted past, neare to my Face, the shapes of things became indistinct, and no Shadow marked the Houre on the Sunne-Dial: a little gust of Wind rose, and stirred the tops of the Trees. The stillnesse of all around was very solemn; a sweete feeling that could not be uttered of lowly Thanksgiving and Love spread over my Heart. The *Lord* was very gratious unto mee; it was a Season of inward Peace, as of outward Silence and Beauty, and my Heart was stirred *as the Trees of the Wood are moved by the Wind.*

Came into the House, and seeing the Sand-glasse that I had turned at Sunne-sett that it was runne out, the Prayer arose that so my Life might runne its course, and gently cease.

FINIS.

PRINTED BY WHITTINGHAM AND WILKINS,
TOOKS COURT, CHANCERY LANE.

www.ingramcontent.com/pod-product-compliance
Lightning Source LLC
Chambersburg PA
CBHW032055220426
43664CB00008B/1015